M000201428

SURVIVING THE STAINED GLASS JUNGLE

MERCER
UNIVERSITY PRESS

*Endowed by*
TOM WATSON BROWN
*and*
THE WATSON-BROWN FOUNDATION, INC.

# *Surviving*

## THE STAINED GLASS JUNGLE

William L. Self

MERCER UNIVERSITY PRESS
MACON, GEORGIA

MUP/P499

© 2011 Mercer University Press
2014 Paperback edition
1400 Coleman Avenue
Macon, Georgia 31207
All rights reserved

First Edition

Books published by Mercer University Press are printed on acid-free
paper that meets the requirements of American National Standard for
Information Sciences—Permanence of Paper for Printed Library
Materials.

Mercer University Press is a member of Green Press Initiative
(greenpressinitiative.org), a nonprofit organization working to help
publishers and printers increase their use of recycled paper and
decrease their use of fiber derived from endangered forests. This book
is printed on recycled paper.
Library of Congress Cataloging-in-Publication Data

Self, William L.
  Surviving the stained glass jungle / William L. Self. -- 1st ed.
     p. cm.
  ISBN 978-0-88146-517-4 (paperback : alk. paper)
  1. Clergy--Appointment, call, and election. 2. Vocation, Ecclesiastical.
3. Pastoral theology. I. Title.
  BV4011.4.S45 2011
  253'.2--dc23
                                2011024689

*To Carolyn*

*My One and Only Love*

# CONTENTS

## ACKNOWLEDGMENTS

*For none of us lives to himself alone and none of us dies to himself alone* (Romans 14:7). It can also be said that no one writes or ministers by himself. I owe a great debt of gratitude to the churches that have trusted me to be their pastor through the years. To the fellow ministers who have served alongside me, I owe a debt that can never be repaid.

Barbara Brown, who worked with me for eighteen years as ministry assistant, has always encouraged me to put these thoughts in writing. After she retired she insisted on editing the material and in doing so made many suggestions that improved it. Thank you, Barbara!

Peggy Stanley, who is now my ministry assistant, has been helpful in making sure that the project came together on time.

Carolyn, my one and only love for over fifty-seven years, has not only walked the road with me, enduring the pain and joy of the calling, but responded eagerly when I asked her to write the chapter on the minister's family. She told the story as only a mother could.

Our grandsons, Carter and Benjamin, (along with their parents, Karen and Bryan) have been most encouraging. While we were together with their parents on a family vacation, they observed me writing one afternoon. When I told them I was writing a book about the ministry, they approved and continued to ask me about it for two years. They called it my "homework." Now I can tell them I have finished my homework.

# INTRODUCTION

I love being a minister. There are times I love it more than others. But like all professions, it has good and bad days. It has rhythms that are different from other professions. In fact, one must see it as a calling and not a profession to make any sense out of it at all. The pastor is always on duty. No one should go into the ministry if he cannot give himself to it every minute of every waking hour. It is a life that is the result of a calling from God to do a special task. If it is purely a vocational choice, it will be abandoned early in the first pastorate, usually with a great deal of bitterness. If it is a calling, then the rough patches are seen in a different light and are endured with more understanding. The fact that the ministry is a calling does not exempt it from certain principles that are easy to comprehend.

Many years ago I tried to play the game of golf. I was not very good at it, but I did learn one simple rule that has carried over to this day: "Keep your eye on the ball." It is a simple rule, but the violation of it will destroy your game. It is the same with ministry. I contend that the ministry is a single-minded profession (or calling, if you will), and that to survive and thrive in it, the minister must diligently work to refrain from "double-mindedness." One cannot give himself heart and soul to one thing while in the back of his mind he cherishes a desire for something very different. I believe that the minister is always tempted to forget the single purpose of his life. We must always be mindful of the difficulty of keeping a tight focus on the conditions of our service.

There is an interesting parallel to the ministry given by Hugh Heclo.[1] He asks us to imagine two baseball players (it could be any game, and I think it applies to the ministry as well as baseball), each equally endowed with athletic ability and a desire to win, and each equally competitive. One he calls Barry, the other Cal. Barry sees himself as being responsible to his fans and the record books, but ultimately to himself. Cal has similar views, but ultimately his supreme obligation is to the game itself. Barry is into succeeding in his athletic career and Cal is into succeeding in the game itself. For Barry, the game is a setting for displaying his athletic skills. For Cal, the game includes the whole rich tradition of people and events that define his performance. The history of the game is a living thing. Barry sees a set of rules, whereas Cal sees an ethos in which the formal rules are just the outer shell of the game. He senses the history of the game, its traditions, passions, and stories. Barry plays to help his team win, but Cal plays for something more than his team. He loves the game and plays it for that reason and that reason alone. But Barry is in love with his own accomplishment.

This is not unlike some ministers. They find success early in the ministry. People come in large numbers to hear them preach, their churches flourish, and they receive accolades from the civic as well as the religious community. Their opinions are sought by politicians and community leaders. Their successes become the northern point on their compasses. Other equally talented ministers may have large congregations as well, but preach not primarily for the love of their own successes, but because they stand in the company of a great cloud of witnesses who have had the sacred privilege of standing at the pulpit through the ages, proclaiming the Gospel. They are surrounded by history, the love of the church, the call of God, and a sense that they are not alone in this undertaking. We need more Cals and fewer Barrys in the ministry today.

During the time I served the West Bradenton Baptist Church in Bradenton, Florida, I invited Dr. Duke McCall, the president of the Southern Baptist Theological Seminary in Louisville, Kentucky, to lead our church in a revival meeting. I was not a graduate of the seminary he led, and he did not know me, or I him, but it seemed right to extend an invitation to him for this event. Each night during the week, after he had finished preaching, we went to our home and Carolyn had a snack prepared for us. Dr. McCall and I would talk into the early morning and then I would take him back to his hotel. On two mornings, Carolyn prepared breakfast for us because we had talked all night long. The conversation revolved around the practical matters relating to being a pastor, and in his case a seminary president. Until this time I had felt guilty about doing the practical things that had to be done before I could do the works of ministry I was called and educated to do. We formed a strong bond that week that extends to the present day. We called those talks "The School for Scoundrels," and the spirit of those all-night conversations is reflected in this book.

It is common for pastors to pull me aside during meetings and ask me to help them with a practical problem or to just give them some encouragement as they deal with difficult people or situations. A frequently asked question is, "How have you been able to survive it for so long?" This book is intended to help other pastors, just as "The School for Scoundrels" helped me.

One further word as we begin. The English language does not have a neutral gender, and it seems artificial to always write his/her when referring to the pastor. So I have chosen to use the masculine form, although I wish to make it clear that I celebrate the new awareness in our churches that God calls both women and men into ministry, and some of our most effective ministers are women. During the time I was their pastor, the Wieuca Road Baptist Church in Atlanta was among the first large Southern Baptist churches to ordain people to ministry without respect to gender. I've paid my dues ... so let us begin.

# 1

## WITH SINGLENESS OF HEART:
## THE CALL TO MINISTRY

It all started with me when I was thirteen. I had always attended the First Baptist Church of Delray Beach, Florida, but because of my friendship with Jim Robinson, the son of the pastor of the First Presbyterian Church, I had started attending their Sunday night program. After all, that was where all the "cool" kids went. For some reason my pastor at First Baptist became concerned about this and came to our house one afternoon urging me to attend the summer assembly for Baptist youth sponsored by the Florida Baptist Convention, which was held on the campus of Stetson University in Deland, Florida. I went, and my life has never been the same. Our group stayed in Conrad Hall, an old dormitory on campus, and for the first time, I was exposed to a world I had never known. There were vibrant Christians from other parts of Florida, strong preachers deeply involved with their young people, exuberant worship services filled with excited young people, and a Baptist church world that was bigger than I had imagined. The experience fed a deep need inside of me.

Each night during the worship time, I sat in the back row of the balcony of the auditorium in Elizabeth Hall, where I could take in the whole experience. After the evening service we walked a few blocks to town and descended on the soda shop, indulging our appetites for ice cream and milk shakes while doing some innocent flirting, knowing that when the week was over we would, in all likelihood, never see each other again. In my case that was not quite true. I became good friends with Met Burgess, who, after college, married my friend George Schrieffer. Later, when I was pastor of the West Bradenton (Florida) Baptist Church, George served with me as Minister of Education. Our families have kept in touch with each other through the years.

Friday night of that week at the conference changed my life. The service concluded with a strong altar call to respond by going forward to stand with others on the stage if you felt the call of God to be a missionary, a preacher, or would answer the call to any other form of full-time Christian service. I went forward. It seemed like a long distance from the back of the balcony to the stage. The building was constructed so that to make that step from the balcony, I had to go outside the room, into the foyer, and then back into the building, but I did not care. I was going to the stage. I was not able to put into words what was going on inside of me, but I knew that it was of God. To this day I have never doubted that experience. This positive sense of God's call has been the definitive experience of my life. During times of depression, opposition, struggle, and anxiety, there was one thing I knew for certain: God had pulled me out of the back row of the balcony of Elizabeth Hall at Stetson University during the Deland Assembly on a Friday night when I was only thirteen. He had made it clear to me that I was to preach the Gospel and that I was to prepare myself in every way for this task.

I felt strange after this. Of course I told my mother, who did not receive the news enthusiastically (preachers are nice, but you do not necessarily want one in your family), nor my pastor, who did not know what to do with me. The church was gracious, but most thought it was just a phase I was going through and would get over before long. A few of the old saints in the church began to see it as their duty to shape the young preacher, and so they showered me with books and advice. One woman in particular, the ultimate "church lady," was on a mission to turn me into an ultra right-wing, fire-breathing, Bob Jones University-style fundamentalist. I disappointed her.

One Sunday evening a few months after the experience at Stetson, the pastor announced to the church that we would be conducting "Youth Week," a program established by the Convention, and all the churches were encouraged to participate. For one week the youth would operate the church under the direction of adult church leaders. Every position would be filled by a young person, including that of pastor. He went on to inform the church that one of their very own young people would be preaching ... Bill Self. That was the first time I had heard anything about this. After the service people began to congratulate me and to pledge to me their prayer support as I prepared to preach my first sermon. I was shocked beyond measure. Immediately after the service, I made my way to the pastor and asked him if I had understood him correctly. "Yes, you did, and I'll help you with your sermon," he assured me. Later he loaned me his copy of a study Bible, and that's the last help I remember him giving.

The assigned night finally arrived. It seemed that everyone was there, and for some reason I do not remember being particularly nervous. Some of my friends from the Presbyterian Church came, as well as many from our local high school. Most came out of curiosity. Our little town did not have much excitement, and this had become a community event. My mother was nearly out of her mind with anxiety. Something happened that night. God was there in an unusual way. I knew it, and the church knew it too. It was as if I had received a special blessing from God, perhaps somewhat like the baptism of Jesus when the Holy Spirit of God descended. I took as my text Daniel 1:8-16, the story of the Hebrew children in exile successfully continuing their proper diet during their captivity. The title was "The Teenager and the Church." That is all I remember, and I do not have my notes from that sermon.

I am confident that it was not the sermon material, nor was it the presentation that confirmed my calling, but rather it was the sense of God's presence in the whole evening. There comes a time where one knows in the deepest part of his being, that, as naïve as it may sound to secular ears, he has been called by God. This was the first of several times I have experienced this confirmation.

That night I slept really well, because I knew what I had been born to do. It was not a profession I had chosen but rather a calling to which I had responded. I had not chosen it … I had been chosen. "Once I was blind, but now I can see," and that's all that mattered. To be in the ministry, it is absolutely necessary to have a strong sense of God's call. If the ministry is only a vocational choice, the minister is doomed from the beginning. No one in his right mind would do this for a living. To do this work, one needs to be out of his own mind and have the mind of Christ.

Since that night, I have relived that experience many times. It confirmed for me the call of God. During the difficult days in school, it gave me a strong sense of purpose. After some deacons' meetings and church business conferences, not to mention Stewardship Committee meetings, I have had to remember that I had been chosen for this task; I did not choose it.

It was natural for me to attend Stetson University. While in high school, I had worked at a local men's clothing store after school and on Saturdays. About the time I was ready to graduate, the owner of the store informed me that he was planning to open another store in the Hollywood Beach Hotel, in Hollywood, Florida. He wanted me to manage it. It was a dream job for a boy of eighteen. I could quick-start my life, bypass college, continue going to church, and be a good layman. I could buy a car, live at home, and see this ministry thing as a passing fad. I made the commitment to my employer in the late spring, and he sent me to a larger store in Fort Lauderdale for training. In the meantime, the church in Delray was planning another Youth Week, and they were using a different speaker each night. I was asked to speak one night during the week. I was terribly conflicted; this ministry thing was over, I thought. I agreed to speak in order to prove to myself that it really was over. The evening was rather flat, and nothing in particular happened during the service, but the next morning when I drove into the parking lot in Fort Lauderdale, it was raining and I was trapped in the car. During that time God spoke to me and I knew I had to go to school and prepare to preach. When the rain stopped, I went in and informed my employer that I could not accept his offer. I was going to school to pursue my calling to preach. Needless to say, he was not happy with my decision. That evening, when I told my mother, she had mixed emotions but was supportive. The next day I began the process of applying to Stetson, which in the 1950s was a much easier task than it is now. In those days, the Florida Baptist Convention had an arrangement with Stetson to pay full tuition for anyone preparing for ministry who would be a cooperating Baptist pastor upon completion of his education. That, along with a small supplement from my father's estate, made it possible for me to begin.

Stetson was a wonderful experience for me, and I plunged right in. Although I did not have a good academic foundation, they were patient with me and I caught up. However, it seemed that every class challenged what I believed. This was not Sunday school. I had my periods of doubt, misunderstanding, and rebellion against the ministry. My case of "intellectual measles" was not as severe as others in my class experienced, but it was enough for me. Also, I did not fit well with others preparing for the ministry. They were more conservative than I was. They were from fundamentalist churches, just as I was, but somehow it did not take with me. They knew when Jesus was returning; they had no question of the literalness of Jonah nor the exact place of women in the churches. They did not attend movies nor eat in restaurants that served alcohol. Of course, they did not use alcohol in any form, and dancing was out of the question. They did not smoke unless they had been in the military. For them, the earth was created in seven twenty-four-hour days, and on and on it went. More than one night I found myself clinging to the one thing of which I was certain ... I had been called by God to preach the Gospel, even though I did not seem to be like the others, who also claimed to have been called by God. In fact, in the deepest part of my soul I knew that this was the reason I had been born. With that assurance I have been able to survive the parish ministry and all the issues surrounding the "stained-glass" culture.

There was a certain irony in the Stetson experience. Adrian Rogers, who later defeated me for president of the Southern Baptist Convention in 1979, and I entered Stetson the same year. He had grown up in West Palm Beach, Florida, at the same time I was in Delray Beach, eighteen miles away. We had played football against each other, although we did not know each other at the time, and had been active in the youth activities sponsored by the Palm Lake Baptist Association. I did not know that Adrian and Joyce Gentry (whom he later married) had entered the Better Speakers Contest sponsored by the Association. I had been preparing for months for the contest. Many of the churches in the Association had young people in the contest, but Joyce, Adrian, and I were the finalists. The finals were held at the First Baptist Church of West Palm Beach, and it was really a big event for the churches. We each made our speeches and waited for what seemed like an eternity for the decision of the judges. Finally, the judges announced that Joyce had won the contest and declared that Adrian and I had tied. Adrian and I later became friends at Stetson, and, although we never agreed theologically, we respected each other. Years later, when he was pastor of the Bellevue Baptist Church in Memphis, and I was at Wieuca Road Baptist in Atlanta, we were on opposite sides of the Southern Baptist war. In 1979 he defeated me for president of the Convention by an overwhelming number of votes. Late at night at the annual meetings of the Convention, we talked together privately in hotel lobbies as old friends on opposite sides. The friendship that had developed during our teen years prevailed. It made the whole difficult issue much more civil. When Adrian was dying of cancer, I wrote to him, and he replied that although we had rarely agreed, he had always respected me and our friendship.

Most churches have their share of difficult people, who, for whatever reason, are quick to criticize, complain, and generally cause the minister pain. I have taken comfort in the observation that the church is like a swimming pool: all the noise is at the shallow end. These people have been very unpleasant to deal with, but they, too, are those for whom Christ died, and He has called me to minister to them particularly. Without a sense of calling, it would have been impossible to do so.

A call is central to an understanding of Christian disciple-ship. In the Bible, a call appears to be a summons to a relationship with God and a commission to a task. God can and does call individuals and groups. In the Hebrew Bible, the people of Israel were chosen for a covenant with God and appointed to be a "light to the nations." The New Testament shows that the church was (is) called to be united with God through the Gospel and sent out as witnesses.

Individuals are called out to be messengers of God's word—Moses before the burning bush, Jeremiah to the captives in exile, Saul on the road to Damascus, to name but a few. In each case there is protest from the one being called, and the assurance from God that He would be with them. Human fear and weakness presents itself, but in each case those called receive the promise of God's protection and strength. This has been my experience, along with the testimony of those who have answered the call and served for any length of time.

God's call is a lifetime experience, and it is difficult to find any satisfaction apart from it. When one understands the call of God, it becomes clear what Paul meant when he said that he was a prisoner of Jesus Christ (Ephesians 4:1).

We minister because we have been called, and the world desperately needs us to do it. In ministering to people, we have a privilege that no one else in our culture has. We are with people in moments of their deepest need, in times of transition, and in moments of their greatest joy. The longer we serve, the more we realize the power of presence, the power of His word, and the power of influence. I have realized as I have grown older that it is a rare privilege to be set apart by God to lead His people.

I also know that at some point I will be asked to give an accounting to God for the way I have led and served His people. My accountability to God is always before me, as it is with all of us. This influences the decisions I must make each day as I go about my duties. On occasion, I have shared this with the congregation from the pulpit. This has helped them see that what we do is not one dimensional, but has an eternal dimension.

# 2

## SQUIRRELS IN THE ATTIC AND WATER IN THE BASEMENT: DEALING WITH CRITICISM

Recently our house was invaded by squirrels. They settled in our attic. After all, it was a great place to build a nice nest, warm in the winter, protected from the rain and snow, and easily accessed. At the same time, because of a builder's error, we had water in our basement. Neither of these problems were life-threatening, and they did not cause me to want to sell the house and move to Australia or seriously consider burning it down. They were a diversion from the main focus of our family life and caused us to use up a lot of emotion and resources in getting them fixed. The irritations of the ministry, especially criticism, are much the same way. They use up energy and resources, divert our attention, and threaten our ability to do our assigned task.

I have long believed that the ministry is the world's most advised profession. From the day I announced to my home church that I was being called into the pastoral ministry, the advice started, not only to me directly, but to my mother as well. "I hope Bill isn't going to be one of those preachers that..." was said so many times to my mother by the women in her Sunday school class, and brought home to me as gospel, that I actually asked her to stop telling me what they had said. There were suggestions about lifestyle, education, marriage, theology, denominational affiliation, and anything else you could imagine. It was told to me, or strongly suggested, what car to drive, which girls to date, what books to read, what clothes to wear, how to comb my hair, which movies not to see (if I went to the movies at all), and on and on it went. When I was doing youth revivals before and during college and seminary, laymen took it upon themselves to take me aside and give me a little "constructive criticism." In almost every case, "constructive criticism" was code for an attack on my personhood. Occasionally, it was preceded by "I mean this in Christian love ...," the sincerity of which I found hard to believe, given the severity of the attack. In each of the churches I have pastored there have been those who were generous with their advice, both for me and my family. I must say that as I grew older, the advice began to lessen. They must have decided I was too old to change my ways.

Early on I faced this issue. After much thought and prayer, I decided on a plan of action. All of the articles on this subject I was able to find said that I should listen to the criticism in order to determine ways I could improve. This did not feel right for me. No one is perfect, but neither could one possess all the flaws I was told I had. If I had done half the things suggested to me, I would have been a severely conflicted person. Almost all of this criticism was directed at my personhood. They were attacking who I was, not what I did. It was an effort to control, not to enhance. Once a person or a group controls the pastor or his family, that person or group has taken control of the church.

It is not an overstatement to assert that every issue comes down to POWER, who has it and who does not. Power is not given up easily, and there are some very sophisticated ways used in churches to take the power from the pastor. Perhaps Nietzsche was right, we do have an essential will to power. If the young pastor can be taught to listen to the critics early in his development, the future churches will have a leader they can control. I have long concluded that there is no such thing as "constructive criticism." Of course, help may be given to all of us, but it should be offered in a way that does not to appear as an attack on our personhood, or as an effort to mold the young minister in the "helper's" own image.

It is very difficult for people to understand the pastorate from the outside. This calling is unique, and until you have been there, it is impossible to explain to anyone who has not seen it from the inside. I have some wonderful laymen as close friends. They have walked with our family through the most difficult territory I ever expect to go through. Their value to me was not trying to explain how a church situation should be handled, but rather in being my friend and giving me support in the midst of the struggle.

Carolyn and I, much to our dismay, have found that even lifelong friends eventually have trouble just being friends with us. Frequently, they feel that they must lecture us on how the preacher should run the church and other related matters. It takes away one of the few outlets we have for just being ourselves and having a good time.

One deacon, in addressing a church problem to me (one which he had instigated), took me to breakfast at a fancy hotel in our neighborhood and informed me that the whole problem in the church was that Carolyn and I were too close to each other. Incidentally, I suggested that he not use this against me in his gossip around the church. The accusation was so ridiculous he would appear to be a fool. Also, I could give him a list of fifty churches that would be glad to have that problem.

I agree with Theodore Roosevelt who said,

> It is not the critic who counts; not the man who points out how the strong man stumbles, or where the doer of deeds could have done them better. The credit belongs to the man who is actually in the arena, whose face is marred by dust and sweat and blood; who strives valiantly; who errs, who

comes short again and again, because there is no effort without error and shortcoming; but who does actually strive to do the deeds; who knows great enthusiasms, the great devotions; who spends himself in a worthy cause; who at the best knows in the end the triumph of high achievement, and who at the worst, if he fails, at least fails while daring greatly, so that his place shall never be with those cold and timid souls who neither know victory nor defeat. ("Citizenship in a Republic," delivered at the Sorbonne in Paris, France, on 23 April 1910)

My seminary education was very special to me. I appreciated my professors as well as the administration. They knew their disciplines well, encouraged excellence and integrity in our work, and evidenced a genuine religious commitment. For the most part, I felt they were teaching because of a sincere calling to the profession. Nevertheless, I found that they all exhibited a naive understanding of the pastorate that bordered on hostility. This was in more than one seminary and over a long period of time. The prevailing thought in seminary seemed to be that if a student was particularly bright, he should teach; if he was sympathetic, he should be a counselor; if he had a gift for administration, he should work for the denomination; if he was very dedicated, he should go to the mission field. All the rest of us could go into the pastorate—not a very affirming suggestion.

In my struggle with the pastorate and how to survive and thrive in it, I consulted all the literature I could find. Several of the books and articles sounded like the advice I was given as a young person by the well-meaning "church ladies" in my mother's Sunday school class except that it was dressed up in better language. In short, it does not take long to know if an author has been there, and if so, is angry about the experience. In some cases it seemed the author was just trying to sell a book. After all, as I have noted earlier, this is the world's most advised profession. Some books on the pastorate appeared to be targeted to the academic community, which is all right, but I needed something that had the smell of the pastorate on it. The blood of deacons' meetings, the tears of the hospital room, the anguish of the graveside, the fear of the building program, the dilemma of having to decide between your son's baseball game and a visit to the hospital in order to quiet a gossiping Sunday school class, and much more seemed to be missing from the literature about the pastorate.

For years I had the privilege of being a weekly guest on a popular morning television program in our city. One particular morning when I arrived at the studio, I was told that I would be interviewing a special guest who was in town to conduct seminars for clergy and other professionals. He was an Ivy League-educated psychologist who was teaching in a prestigious school in the New York area. Before we went on camera, in order to get to know him, I asked what he had to teach clergy and why I should encourage them to attend his seminar. He was indignant and implied that clergy were a needy group of people who did not understand human dynamics. After further conversation, I tried to explain to him before we went on the air a little bit about what clergy faced each day. He would hear nothing of it. He had all the answers and clergy should listen to him. I did ask, in my frustration, if we had a conference for psychologists to help them understand clergy, would he attend. "Absolutely not," he replied. On the air I tried to be helpful, but he did not know or understand clergy, and this was clear to even the most casual viewer. In some way he was a microcosm of the culture in which we live. The population in general, as well as in the church, has a very shallow understanding of the work of the pastor.

My mail and emails are filled each week with those who are promoting some seminar or event. They have the answer. Again,

I concluded that the ministry is the world's most advised profession. Why not a book written by a veteran minister of over fifty years in the active pastorate, churches of all sizes and composition, and through issues beginning with the race struggles of the 1950s through the consumerism of the twenty-first century?

I was asked to address an insurance convention in St. Louis, Missouri, several years ago. The audience was composed of about one thousand sales people for the host company. While sitting on the dais waiting for my turn to speak, the president of the company turned to me and asked, "Who are you?"

"I'm your speaker for today," I replied.

"What do you have to say to us?" he asked.

I said, "Each week I have to attract about two thousand people of diverse ages, education, and interest to one piece of real estate, persuade them to contribute ten percent of their income consistently to our church, and lead a staff of over 100 people with no clear lines of authority and no product to sell. I do all of this by persuasion. *Now*, do I have anything to say to your sales force?"

"I think you do," he replied.

Even though you know in your mind that criticism is a normal part of being a pastor, it is not pleasant to receive, nor is it helpful for the church. So what do you do about it? I have several suggestions that have served me well through the years.

If I have a particularly vocal or destructive critic, who may or may not have turned into an opponent, I seek to locate and identify the circle of friends this person has in the church. Then I make sure I have a solid relationship with them. You do not necessarily have to explain to them the tension between yourself and the trouble-maker. They just need to feel like they know you and know that you are their friend. This isolates the critic. In almost every case, the critic is not able to light a fire in them that will burn you and weaken or destroy your ministry or damage the church. I developed this strategy while watching a news report about forest fires in the western part of the United States. The firefighters would light controlled fires ahead of the forest fire in order to starve it by burning with the control fire the fuel it would need. This is called "backfiring," and it has worked well for me.

Another technique that has served me well is to meet with the chairman of our deacon body at least once a week. When Dr. Rayburn Fisher, president of a savings bank in our city and former superintendent of schools for a county in Alabama, was nominated to be chairman of our deacons, he had one condition that had to be met before he agreed to take the job: he wanted a meeting with the pastor every week. This seemed a little over the top for me, but I agreed to it because I wanted Dr. Fisher to be our chairman. We varied the place and time of meeting, adjusting it to suit our schedules. At the end of his term, I determined it had been the best thing I could have done. He knew my heart, and I knew his. He interpreted what we were doing to the congregation, and this kept down much criticism and misunderstanding. I have continued this practice through the years and consider it to be a valuable tool for informing the congregation as well as the leadership of the church in a very subtle and informal manner. Also, after several years of this, the pastor develops a group of leaders that he has prayed with, planned with, and who understand and protect him. Several past chairmen have said that they would miss the weekly meeting and prayer time with the pastor when their terms were over and asked if they could continue with it.

There are times when a more direct approach to criticism is required. This is very tricky. The weekly meeting with the chairman helps to clarify the issues and to see them through other eyes. It also gives you the chance to assess any unseen dangers that may be present. If your approach to the problem backfires, there is someone to help you face the resulting situation. I have found that if you let a situation simmer for a while in the church, there is peace for a short time, but during that time the problem grows larger and much more difficult to manage or solve. If, on the other hand, the problem is addressed in its infancy, there may be an explosion of some sort, but then the problem usually goes away. I have learned the hard way to never, never, never take the problem into the pulpit. While the problem is present in the church, the pastor should do his best preaching.

The concept of a regularly scheduled meeting with the deacon chairman led to two other meetings that have helped to keep the church free from excessive criticism. I remembered that Jesus had said that, "My Father's house will be called a house of prayer for all people" (Matt. 21:13). So before any activity begins on Sunday morning, I have invited all who want to attend to a prayer meeting with the pastor. We meet for thirty minutes and the attendance varies, but we share our deepest needs and the needs of our congregation and pray for power in worship and Sunday school. The power of corporate prayer is evident, and a group of people know the pastor's heart and are praying for the presence of the Holy Spirit in the time of teaching as well as the worship service. This meeting is open to all and has proven effective at keeping us on the same agenda while having a spiritual impact on those praying and those for whom we are praying.

I also meet with all ministerial staff early on Sunday morning. This seems to be such a simple thing, but I have had to constantly remind them of the importance of the meeting. No coach would take a team onto the field without first meeting with his coaches before the game. The meeting is quick and well planned. We check our watches (you'd be surprised at the difference in time between watches), talk about any special programs occurring that day, have a report on any who may be joining the church that Sunday, walk through the worship service, and pray for the day. All this can be done in fifteen minutes. Our congregation knows of this staff meeting and respects that we value the day so much that we have a last-minute check of the plans and pray before we begin the day. I believe that when the people know that this day is special to us as leaders of the congregation, they will not take their responsibilities lightly. We are modeling for the church. This has helped to keep the squirrels out of our attic and the water out of our basement. The influence of these meetings slowly moves through the congregation. It is preventive maintenance.

Although preventive maintenance is best, there are times when a direct conversation with the critic is necessary. There is no strict rule as to when this should be done, or how it is to be done, but through very painful trial and error I have come to some conclusions.

People whom you are counseling cannot be trusted. When you are working with a person through some very difficult areas in their lives, the pastor is sworn to confidentiality. I found out early in the ministry that the counselee is not necessarily held to that same code of honor. He can say what he pleases about the session with the pastor to whomever he wishes, but the pastor is duty bound to protect the substance and confidentially of the counseling session. On more than one occasion, I have been betrayed by the counselee who misrepresented to his circle of friends what was said in confidence in the session. I once had an alcoholic tell his friends that I had encouraged him to drink all he wanted to drink, that rehab would be a waste of his time, and that he was above such measures.

I never do any counseling without a secretary or another responsible person sitting in the outer office. If I am working with a child, I have the parents with me in the room, or at least have someone outside. I also decided not to have a couch in my office. Instead, I have large club chairs that provide comfortable seating that is in no way suggestive. All of our rooms in the church, as well as the offices, have glass windows in them. I strongly believe we must avoid the very appearance of evil, particularly in the light of recent news reports concerning the misuse of the pastoral office and child abuse and molestation.

I also decided not to ever have lunch with a female without a third party present. I have been accused of being very old-fashioned and out-of-date because of this, but it has given my wife and church comfort, and me a level of protection. One young lady in our church was going through a divorce because of her husband's infidelity. She asked that I have lunch with her to talk about the situation. When I told her that I needed a third party present before I could do this, she was at first very indignant, but then she told me that after thinking about it, she understood and appreciated my position, particularly in light of her problem. My wife Carolyn joined us for lunch.

This is also true of any direct conversation one may have with a church member concerning his or her criticism. It is not out of the question to have a third party present in the room when you have this direct conversation. The critic will not like it, but this person doesn't like anything else that you are doing, so what is there to lose? When I have used this procedure, it has been when I thought all other avenues to understanding were closed.

It is not unusual to have people wish to change the theology of the church to fit the theology they have acquired in a private Bible study, or from reading a book offered by a popular television preacher, or a session they have attended at a conference conducted by a person(s) with a strong personality but dubious credentials. It is much easier to steal a church than it is to build one, and there are always people ready to steal your church. They always attack the pastor. Their hope is to weaken his leadership and makes it easier for them to lead the congregation astray.

I once had three very popular young adult families meet with me and inform me that they were on a mission to make our church a charismatic church, and that they would do it with or without me. I informed the formal and informal leadership of our church about their intent, and after subsequent meetings with them, their movement was stopped and they left the church.

Another time I had to confront several families who were intent on changing our theology. They had come under the influence of a popular speaker on the family who advocated that the husband should rule his house with an iron fist, and only he could speak to God on behalf of the family. They could only go to God through the father. "Submissive womanhood" was their rallying cry. One of these ladies came to me and literally pounded on my desk while shouting, "You don't preach submissive womanhood; you're a heretic!" I replied, "You don't seem very submissive." She paused, thought a moment, and then replied. "I've found that I can control from a submissive posture." It was not long after that she and her husband divorced.

I am convinced that most church troublemakers are struggling with difficulties in their own lives and are using the church as a way of dealing with their own personal demons. During an especially stressful time at Wieuca Road Baptist Church, the church had been worked into a frenzy over some long-forgotten issue by several families and older singles who had joined forces. Before the night that this was scheduled to be discussed in a business meeting, one of the leaders of this group, who happened to be an older single, asked to see me before the meeting. He insisted on a private meeting. After we had a short discussion of the issues, he stood and said to me, "Bill, if you will embrace me now as a Christian brother, I'll call off the opposition in the meeting tonight, and we will have a peaceful church." I was stunned. Had he created all of this trouble because he wanted affirmation? What should I do? It would be easy to buy him off with an insincere embrace. I felt like Jesus on the Mount of Temptation: "Bow down and worship me and I'll give you the kingdoms of this world," said the devil. Right or wrong, I would not be manipulated into a cheap gesture of affirmation. He had demonstrated to me how troubled he actually was. I stood and took his hand and said, "I'll pray for you and for God's church," and so I did. He left my study, went straight to the meeting, and caused a lot of trouble. I have often wondered if I handled it correctly. What would you have done?

Others have tried to enlist the church to support questionable or ill-conceived ministry projects in the community or to support a political candidate of their choice ... and on it goes. When you are protecting the life and nature of the church, the pastor must use any legitimate means to protect the flock. Everyone wants the pastor to hitch the church to his or her cause. As pastors, we have one thing that is more valuable than anything else: a constituency. Many want to use it for purposes that are not necessarily God's purpose. They are perfectly happy to let you build the flock, pay the bills, do the maintenance, and let them hook the flock up to their cause. We must remember that we are stewards of the flock of God, and one day we will be required to give an accounting of our stewardship. If the church is attached to anything other than the Gospel of Jesus Christ and His resurrection, it is not as God created it. When the substitute cause fails, and it will, the church will go down with it, or at least be severely damaged.

Preventive maintenance is better than trying to fix a problem after it has grown large. Committee meetings are a trouble for every pastor. Most of us do not like church work (committee meetings) but love the work of the church (preaching, teaching, missions, and evangelism). These meetings are hard work and potentially very dangerous. Helping people see the importance of your vision, or having initiatives shot down by someone who does not have the wisdom necessary to serve on the committee in the first place, is painful beyond words. I agree with the wag who said that a camel is a horse designed and built by a church committee. However, these meetings are necessary and should be seen as the price we pay to do this work. I have developed a strategy for these meetings that has helped keep down undue stress for me and the church. It seems so simple that I hesitated at first to include it.

In many meetings the pastor must convince reluctant committee members of the wisdom of his proposal under consideration. There is a natural inclination to resist any initiative when we first hear of it in a meeting. Also, some church members are reluctant to oppose their friends and neighbors who may be on the committee. After all, these neighbors will be with them long after the pastor has moved to another place of service. In short, this can be a place where much scarring can occur. I try to arrive at the meeting early and greet individuals personally as each one arrives. I engage in small talk as much as I can with them before the meeting begins. Small talk is not trivial—it is a form of stroking, or relationship-building. It helps remove any barriers that may exist. Dr. Duke McCall, longtime president of Southern Baptist Theological Seminary in Louisville, Kentucky, was a brilliant leader and master strategist. I watched him use this skill to perfection. The pastor does not want anyone to go home and report that he would not talk to them. As childish as this may seem, I've seen more than one pastor fall victim to this immaturity in his congregation.

Remember that in church work, the pastor rarely has an

opportunity to address his critics directly. They usually shoot from the cover of anonymity. They also triangulate; that is, they get someone else, a third party, to carry their complaint or criticism. I count it a rare privilege to be able to sit down with a person who does not agree with me and have an open discussion on the issues. It is not uncommon for people to ambush the pastor as he walks down the hall of the church going to teach or preach. They demand an answer on the spot. If possible, I get them to see that I can give them more attention if they will make time to see me in the office during the week.

If I get a letter or email with a complaint in it, I try to answer it the same day, if possible. Usually, the fact that I answered it, even if the answer was not to his satisfaction, is helpful. This opens the door to "agree to disagree" and to do it agreeably. Incidentally, I never write a letter or email that I would not have printed on the front page of the *Atlanta Journal-Constitution*. Also, I have instructed my secretary to never put an anonymous letter on my desk. They are to be thrown away as soon as they are opened. If the writer will not sign it, I will not read it. This has been announced to the church as well.

Nineteenth-century clergyman Phillips Brooks once received an anonymous letter that had only the word "FOOL" written in large letters across the page. He took it to the pulpit, held it up, and announced that he had received many letters that were unsigned, but that this was the first one he had received that had been signed with no letter included!

As a part of this committee initiative, I have found that my primary function is much more subtle than that of being a promoter of programs, although that is what is usually seen by the congregation. I discovered early that my primary role was that of pastor. Regardless of the results of the meeting, I was still their pastor. I must speak pastorally, for who knows when I will be called to their hospital room to minister to them, or when I will meet them at the funeral home when tragedy strikes, or have the joy of uniting their daughter in marriage. It must be emphasized that the argument is not as important as the person. It is more important to win the person than the argument. The challenge is to do this without sacrificing your integrity.

It startled me to learn that many on committees made it clear to their friends that they had been with the pastor recently, and because of this they could assure any of their friends who were critics of the pastor, or of the church, that they knew the pastor's heart and that his vision for the church was correct. When I came to this realization, my focus in meetings shifted. I did not have to win everything, just the critical things. In fact, it was good for them to see me lose a vote on occasion. It is not good to win all the time. If a pastor insists on winning all the time, he will soon find that that the tide will turn against him. Pick the times and issues that don't mean as much and give them over to the other point of view.

I have said this assuming that the pastor has saturated the issues with prayer. More issues are resolved on our knees than any other way. While playing in the surf at the beach on vacation with our family, I noticed that rarely was there ever a time of perfect calm. If this calm occurred, it was not for long. When my grandchildren had handled one wave, another one, usually bigger, would come. Some would knock us down, and some we would survive still standing. Some would be large, some small. We seemed to enjoy the larger ones. If we had a lot of big ones, we bragged about it at dinner and congratulated ourselves on being able stand up to the larger challenges. It felt like church all over again.

# 3

## THE LONELIEST PERSON IN THE SANCTUARY

The alarm goes off sharply at five o'clock each Sunday morning, and it's time to go through the routine again. Even though I have become more of a morning person as I have grown older, there is something difficult about getting up this early when you know that your neighbors are sleeping soundly. When they do get up, they'll walk the dog, read the paper, have a late breakfast, and, if so inclined, they will get dressed and attend church. If you see them at church, they will want you to be sure to end the service exactly at twelve o'clock so they can get on with their lives.

When I meet them in worship, they will never know the price my family, the church staff, and I have paid to ensure that they have a good day at church. There have been hours of prayer and study, preparation by the worship leaders, the custodians, and some very dedicated lay leaders. This is done as an act of worship itself. When the call to worship is sounded and our time of worship begins, they will gather. They are the ones who did not do at least one of five other things available to them, such as going to their second homes, taking that needless weekend trip, joining their children in one of a hundred activities that our culture has put together to compete with the worship hour, or having nothing else to do. Also, each Sunday you will face a certain number of church shoppers who have come to check you out, not to mention those who see church as free religious entertainment on Sunday morning. This makes up a portion of the congregation each of us must face week after week. You can be sure that the casual attendee will also expect the church to be full of people and energy on the one Sunday a quarter they attend. "What's happening to us, Pastor? It doesn't seem the same as it did last year."

When I look out at the people, I see many things that give me some joy, some hope, and some despair. There is the wife who has just received word that her husband has another interest. There is the husband sitting in the balcony with the other interest. There is the couple who just received word that their son is gay, and the young family that is fighting cancer in their two-year-old daughter. On the other side of the church is the family that lost their home because the bank would not work with them, and the retired couple whose retirement income is disappearing while the officers of the company he worked for all of his life retire with large, obscene bonuses … and on it goes. I see the cancer patient who hopes to get into a trial program for a new drug and the businessman who just lost his business and is too old to start over. There is also the family whose prodigal son has come home, and the young girl whose lab test has come back negative. Don't forget the over-age, out-of-work executive who just got a job at Wal-Mart and the middle-aged doctor who has given up her lucrative suburban practice to spend the rest of her life working in a mission hospital in Ghana "because Jesus has called me to do it."

Some of them need to hear the comfort of God, while others need to hear the wrath of God. Some need encouragement, some need to change their ways. It is all out there. In the first row is the faithful grieving family whose newly married daughter, consumed by alcohol and drugs, has come home to live with them. There is the old couple who love the church but wish it was like it was fifty years ago when they started attending. "Why can't we sing the old songs?"

I have seen the ecclesiastical power brokers working the foyer as the service is beginning. They are the ones who usually decide when it is time to get a new preacher or think the budget is too high. Let's not forget the super-patriot who wants the church to support his political party, just like the pastor on television does, and is going to move heaven and earth to make sure you do. "You never preach on (you name it)."

In every service there are those who are genuinely seeking answers and looking for some hope, and those whose pain is greater than they can bear. There is the young family that has just buried their child because of SIDS. On more than one occasion I have looked at my sermon notes and wondered how any sermon, or even any passage of scripture, for that matter, can speak to all of these people and all of these needs. What should I say and do? If I speak to one group, I will hurt the other. I am the loneliest person in the sanctuary.

We must do this regardless of how we feel or what we have faced personally. Your wife may be sick, but the show must go on. Your children need their father (mother) this morning, but the show must go on. You have spent all of Saturday night in the emergency room with a sick child, but the show must go on. If you happen to miss a Sunday because of something personal, "Pastor, I brought my neighbor to church and you were not there."

This is not a one-time experience; if I get through it this week, I'll face it again next week. How I'd love to be a brick layer! At least at the end of the day he can count the bricks he has laid and measure the wall and know what he has accomplished. Maybe that's why preachers are so aggressive to count attendance and the offering. That is one thing we can count.

The people need us. They cannot express it clearly, but they need us, and somewhere deep within them, they know it. Sometimes they do not know how to relate to us. One lady saw me at the grocery store checkout line with a few things Carolyn had asked me get on the way home, and she said, "Well, I guess you have to have these things just like the rest of us." Others do not know how to react to sermons. I have had people speak to me at the door after a service and say, "Well, Preacher, you didn't have it today," only to be followed by someone with tears streaming down his cheeks who could only say, "Thank you. That sermon saved my life."

Ministry is harder than it seems even for those of us who are trained for it. I have often been angry with God, particularly after visiting a home that has experienced extreme tragedy, and found that the old clichés did not satisfy either them or me. Honesty would not let me repeat them. Just sitting there with them seemed so inadequate, surely I could do something else for them. When people look to you for some answer, some reason for tragedy, some sense in a senseless situation, you do not have anything to say nor do that will unravel it. At least the doctor can give a pill. On more than one occasion I have returned to my study and railed at God. He has called us to stand for Him in senseless situations, but He gives us no word, no help. He seems to be somewhere else. This is an impossible situation, and we are in it alone. That's the rub, and that makes you the loneliest person in the sanctuary.

You have heard a word from the Word and have learned to take succor from it, but after all, you have spent your life studying it. They have spent their lives fixing computers or raising kids. They have never read the great theologians, and they don't hear one on Sunday morning at eleven o'clock either. JEDP means nothing to them, nor should it. That's for the elitists, the specialists, and those who are looking for a reason not to believe. Many of our people are like the mouse caught in the trap— they'll give up the cheese if they can get out of the trap. Life has many of them trapped. "Preacher, do you have any word from

God today?" their faces say. That makes you the loneliest person in the sanctuary.

There are several ways through this dilemma. You could emotionally push back and not put so much of yourself into the church. If they don't care any more than they seem to, then why should I care? They can have about as much church as they want, and it appears that they don't want much church. Your integrity will not let you do that. It would be a lot easier if you could get a job working for the denomination or a university doing something related to the ministry, such as being a chaplain or teacher, or, God forbid, a development officer. Anything to get your life back and to get this ministry thing, this "call" thing, satisfied.

There is another kind of loneliness that faces all leaders. In which direction should I lead them? What kind of church shall we be? How shall we relate to the community? What kind of worship should we have? What kind of staff will we call? How do I rid us of incompetent staff? Should I stay, or should I seek another position? And on it goes. Ultimately, no one can make these and a myriad of other decisions except the pastor.

There comes a time in the life of every pastor in which he is forced to make some decisions. If I stay in this work and fulfill this call, I'll have to get really serious about it. I really need to be more religious. Faith must become more than the sum total of what I have learned in school. I must be more than the manager of an ecclesiastical store. I must start living by what I profess. If I don't eat the food I serve to my people, why should they? Once that line is crossed, you become a minister of the Gospel.

Jesus, on the night He was betrayed, left the upper room and crossed the brook Kedron and went into the Garden of Gethsemane. Sometime we all must cross the brook Kedron if we are to fulfill this calling, and the decision to do this comes after we have embarked on the journey of ministry, not in the initial stages. Ordination cannot do this for you, another degree cannot do it, a bigger church will not do it, nor will another church position. It happens in the heart, "Lord, I'm yours ... wherever You lead I'll go ... and I'll do it without reservation or stipulation." It may mean Africa or Haiti, or it may mean this little forgotten group of dysfunctional people who need me. But I'm yours. That makes you the loneliest person in the sanctuary.

It happened to me this way. After I crash-landed at Wieuca Road Baptist Church after serving there twenty-six years, I had a rush of excitement. I'm free at last! Now that this ministry thing is over I can get on with my life. A good job in the financial world opened to me, and I eagerly took it. If I can lead a church and raise money for buildings and programs, I can surely sell financial products, or manage a group selling them. This would mean that I had my weekends back, and I could have a casual Sunday just like my neighbors. Also, I could visit churches and give advice to the pastors.

It was not that satisfying. Just like Jonah in the belly of the beast, I found that He would not leave me alone. There was a deep hunger inside of me that could not be satisfied. I missed the late-night phone calls. "Pastor, I need to talk to you." No one seemed to need me anymore. There is nothing so out of step as a pastor doing secular work. There is nothing so useless in the secular world as a theological degree. We may be good in the pulpit, but we are lousy in the pew. One night in my study, I was trying to organize some books, and the despair hit me. I could make a good living doing what I was doing. I could have a respectable life selling these products and managing this company, but this was not it for me. I was made for something else. No one would really care if I lived or died, except my immediate family. That night I knew I heard His voice, "I made you to preach." I knew I had to come back.

The little First Baptist Church of Chamblee called and asked if I would be their interim pastor. They were small, and I had had other churches inquire about me being with them as they looked for a pastor, but there was something special about Chamblee. To my surprise they were a very well organized church that had suffered the misfortunes that come to a church in a community that is undergoing severe change. After having struggled to minister to the people around them, and they accomplished a great deal, they could see that the age of their leadership and the changing demographics of the community would dictate their future, and it was not pretty.

The change to Chamblee was refreshing for me. They gave me something that my former church did not know how to give. They loved me back to spiritual health. The dear little blue-haired ladies would come up to me after the service and get under my arm and greet me. Their makeup always left a stain on my suits. I loved the stains; they said something to me. The people trusted their pastor, and that felt good. I vowed again to be sure to never violate that trust.

Before, I had a staff around me to do my every bidding. Now I had the keys to the church and was responsible for opening and closing the building before meetings. Before, I had someone to do the pastoral care (the traffic and hospitals in Atlanta are a killer), but now I had that sole responsibility. I was again doing weddings and funerals. It felt good. I was back! In fact, after they extended the call to me, I was so excited to be back that as I backed the car out of the garage going to the office for the first time, I forgot to push the automatic door opener and backed into the garage door! Carolyn laughed. The loneliness of the sanctuary is not nearly as difficult as not having a pulpit and not being responsible for some group of God's people. I was glad to be the loneliest person in the sanctuary.

I do not know of a way to get rid of that deep, bone-shattering loneliness that comes to you as you see your responsibility for God's people. There is some joy and a sense of accomplishment as you assess the changes in them. Satisfaction comes when a building program is completed (I've had fourteen of them), and you see the mission projects take shape. The life that has been changed or stabilized or liberated is a comforting thing. Of course, there are some failures, but there are some wonderful things that have happened if you have eyes to see.

I have no sage advice for dealing with it. I do not think there is anything new that can be done except to accept it and thank God you have a family to provide support, even though they did not ask to be in a minister's family. I now understand that in spite of the loneliness, the satisfaction of the pastorate far outweighs the isolation experienced in any other profession. I truly believe that on any given Sunday, the pastor experiences more of life and its excitement in one day than most people experience in a lifetime. In moments of extreme loneliness I have felt that God has sent His ministering angels to comfort and guide.

Sunday is coming and the usual preparations are being made; the usual sense of dread and anticipation is running through your body. The questions are always there: Will the people come? Will God speak? Will the offering be enough to pay the bills? A professional football coach only plays sixteen to twenty games a year; your team plays fifty-two. It's demanding, but once you've tasted the unspeakable joy that this work can provide, you will always be glad you have been called to be the loneliest person in the sanctuary. The alarm goes off; it's five o'clock Sunday morning. What will God do with His people this week?

# 4

## ON BEING PURSUED BY THE BLACK DOG:
## DEALING WITH DEPRESSION AND BURNOUT

Do you ever feel that you are the only person trying to do the work of the Lord and that He is hiding from you, He has forgotten you? Do you ever feel trapped at the bottom of a dirty well? Is the black dog of depression always nipping at your heels and you cannot run fast enough to escape?

That's what Winston Churchill called it, the black dog, and it was a condition he experienced often. Many of our finest statesmen and preachers have suffered this condition known as depression. Charles Spurgeon devoted an entire chapter to it in his *Lectures to My Students*, calling it "his fainting fits." When Abraham Lincoln was practicing law, he was so plagued by this that he was reported to have been sitting in the corner of the courtroom before a trial, shaking with depression. Luther, reports Spurgeon, was often in the "seventh heaven of exultation and frequently on the borders of despair."[2] It seems a contradiction that those of us who bring the light and the word of redemption must often walk in darkness.

I have had this difficulty for most of my adult life. Before I had the opportunity to get far into my studies at Stetson, I found that some days it was difficult to get out of bed and get going, although I cannot remember a time that I yielded to it and avoided my work because of it. On into the seminary years and into the pastorate, the issue followed me. It was worse in the first church I served. The church was tough, and there were the pressures of building a building, reorganizing a church that did not want to reorganize, starting our family, plus the pressure of limited finances and opportunities for service beyond our church that would hopefully advance the Kingdom and my career. Frequently at denominational meetings, those on the agenda would be pushing their program and continually say, "The pastor is the key." They made me feel that I was the key to everything, and the pressure was overwhelming. I could list more.

Carolyn was patient with me, even as I was prone to overwork and overeating. In order to deal with this, we would sometimes leave town for an overnight trip. One time a dear friend of ours kept our boys so that we could run away to New York City for a week. Our house was near a cemetery, and Carolyn and I would take long walks in the quiet of the dead. At least I did not have to raise these dead as I had to do in church. None of these tactics cured me of the darkness.

I believe to a large extent these fainting spells are a chosen behavior. Many have argued with me at that point, but the whole idea behind Cognitive Therapy is to deal with issues like this as chosen behavior. I hasten to acknowledge that there are those cases that are much deeper and require a different type of therapy. However, very few people have time or resources to spend on digging into every life experience in order to explain human behavior. I believe with the Cognitive Therapist that if we change the behavior, we will change the feeling. "You can act your way into a new way of feeling easier than you can feel your way into a new way of acting." Some have called this feeling the "common cold" of mental health.

Somewhere I learned to deal with pressure by stepping into "depression," and it protected me for a while, becoming an automatic subconscious response on my part. Although it served me well for a very short time, in the long run it began to interrupt my life and important relationships with family, friends, and congregation.

A vivid experience brought this into clear focus for me. One Friday night I came home from the office, having had a very stressful time dealing with staff and impossible church members. I had promised Carolyn and our two boys, who at the time were about eight and ten years old, that we would go to the mall for dinner and then to a movie. When I drove into the garage, I was greeted by a happy family ready to enjoy an evening together.

"We can't go out tonight," I said. "It's been a horrible day, and, frankly, I'm very depressed."

Carolyn didn't miss a beat. "That's okay," she said. "You stay home and enjoy your depression, and we'll go on to the movie."

And they did. That really angered me and compounded my feelings of depression. I had no recourse but to bury my depression in peanut butter. If you are not aware of the glories of peanut butter for the depressed, you have missed something. A large jar of Jif and a tablespoon can soon take all of your troubles away except, of course, in the aftermath of this assault on your esophagus and stomach. Later that evening when the family returned, I was in bed feeling sorry for myself. The boys came running back to the bedroom.

"Daddy, we're back! We had a great time. Did you enjoy your depression?" That got to me.

After the boys were settled for the evening, Carolyn and I had a long talk. She said," I can't be your wife and your therapist. Take your choice. I'll help you get help with your mood swings and depressions, but we can't keep ignoring them. What shall it be?" I chose to get well. Since that day, I (or both of us together) have been seeing someone regularly for an emotional and mental health tune-up. Everyone else has a pastor, why shouldn't the pastor have one? Several years later, when we established a counseling center at the Wieuca Road Baptist Church, the committee in charge of the center made it possible for our counselor to have regular sessions with another counselor for the same reason. It seems only right for the pastor, who is under great pressure, to have the same support.

During this time I tried to read everything I could on the subject. One popular book on depression was making its way through the church community. I bought it, read about half of it, and literally threw it against the wall in disgust. It was obvious that the author had never been depressed. It was like hearing your mother cuss; the words were right but the feeling was wrong. Depression is the most requested subject when I am invited to other places to speak. I am convinced that more human suffering results from depression than any other disorder. The ancients called it *melancholia*, or a feeling of thick heavy blood in the veins. It manifests itself as a distressed mood, a wish to die, a loss of self-esteem, or delusions of having done a terrible thing. No class or profession is free of it.

"Sometimes I'm up, sometimes I'm down ... O, yes, Lord" (Negro spiritual).

There are times when I find myself being engulfed by a cloud of depression, and I consciously ask myself, "Do you want to get well by fighting off this thing, or do you want to just surrender and enjoy it, and make everyone around you miserable?"

One of our church members reported to me that she had gone to her psychiatrist with this problem, hoping to get some medicine for it. He asked her this simple question, "Do you want me to give you some medicine, or do you want to get well?" I think we all must answer this question.

# 5

## IT'S OKAY TO BE OKAY:
## THE PASTOR'S OWN SELF-CARE

When our boys were about eight and ten years of age and the dollar was very strong in Europe, I got the idea to buy a new German automobile at the factory in Germany. This was a program promoted strongly by the manufacturer. After a visit to my banker and the local agency for the company, I was off to Germany with the family. It was going to be a great adventure for us. We had planned to be in Europe for two weeks enjoying our new auto before shipping it back to the United States.

When we arrived at the factory, we presented our credentials to the receptionist, were told to wait in the well-appointed guest lounge until we heard our name called, and then we would be introduced to our new car. It was not long before we heard our named called over the public address system and an attendant came to escort us to the waiting auto. We walked into a special garage, and there it was, in all of its glory, ready for us to drive away. I was mistaken. Standing next to the car was a rather imposing German dressed in a special uniform who informed us that he needed to explain some things to us about the vehicle before I could take possession of it, and then he started. Our boys looked on in amazement as he began at the back bumper and explained everything about the auto until he got to the front bumper. This intensive introduction took about forty minutes.

The strongest part of the instruction was when he began talking about maintenance. The first service must be performed at 600 miles; this was nonnegotiable. In fact, he was so emphatic about it that all of us thought that the car would self-destruct if this service was not performed. After we finished the instruction and had packed our luggage, we started driving on a beautiful summer day through the marvelous countryside of Germany and Austria. The boys did not see anything, for their eyes were on the odometer. They were afraid the car would not survive if I carelessly overlooked my responsibility to get it serviced. We arrived in a beautiful Austrian village on Saturday evening with 550 miles on the speedometer. They panicked. Tomorrow was Sunday, no one would work on the car tomorrow, and we would be over our limit by Monday. I had no choice but to find a garage that would perform the service on short notice. This would benefit the car and bring peace of mind to our family. Incidentally, I drove that car for eighteen years and had nearly 200,000 miles on it before I sold it. Perhaps there is something to servicing your car regularly.

If this is true for machinery, why not the human body and spirit? This experience became the impetus for Carolyn and me to stop long enough to think through our lives and ministry. We determined to get in charge of ourselves so that that we could serve our people better and have a more meaningful life together. So much of the lore of ministry has to do with sacrifice, martyrdom, and self-denial. The heroes of the faith are thrown into the lions' den, crucified upside down, imprisoned for long stretches of time, but not much is said about taking care of yourself so that you can serve longer and better, keeping your mind fresh so that you can think straighter, or making sure that your body is well-serviced and maintained so that it will not wear out before its time. A tired and beat-up pastor will not grow spiritually or professionally. I don't remember hearing one word about this in seminary.

No church I have served has ever suggested that I take care of myself. The casual church member does not understand the rhythm and demands of ministry life and secretly thinks that we only work one or two days a week anyway. There is little appreciation for study and thinking in most churches. I negotiated a sabbatical leave in one church, and as it came time for me to take it, it was clearly suggested to me by the powers that be that we were in a building program and the church could not afford for the pastor to be away for his vacation time, much less an additional month for study. Add to this the experience of other pastors I had observed. When they returned from their study leave, they had to fight for their jobs because rebellion had broken out in the ranks in their absence. Incidentally, when Moses was on the mountain receiving the Ten Commandments, the people began worshiping the golden calf, and when Jesus was on the Mount of Transfiguration, the disciples left below began to argue among themselves because they were unable to cure a sick child.

Naively, I tried to teach my first church about the role of the pastor. The denomination had a program in which all churches were encouraged to study a book of the Bible simultaneously. My first year there, the Bible study books were 1 and 2 Timothy. This was the perfect text to teach the church what the Bible said about pastoral leadership. They would have none of it. It went against their cultural understanding of the church and its ministry. This is interesting in light of the fact that they claimed to be a biblically based church. I learned there that when culture and the Bible clash, culture usually wins the first round.

Carolyn and I faced the fact that our care was our responsibility. We thought then, as now, that too many pastors want the church to take this responsibility. They wait for a deacons' committee or some informal group to provide a way for them to get some rest or to pay their way to a retreat or conference. In short, many pastors want to be cared for or rescued, as the case may be, and become terribly distressed when the church does not do it.

Compounding this, some pastors' families have no real life of their own, but live on the fringes of one or two prominent families in the church. We could not expect others to do it for us, nor could we live on the fringes of other people's families. This is an artificial way to live. Though we served good people, and they generally wished us well, they could not be expected to rescue us in our times of stress. They had their own stress. I have never been asked by my medical doctor to give him permission to take care of himself. Physician (pastor), heal thyself!

For my money, depression and burnout are the same thing, although the technically minded may be able to separate them. Perhaps burnout is pre-depression, or the front porch to depression. But for this discussion I see them as one and the same. Perhaps burnout is depression-lite.

Those of us in the helping professions are most susceptible to it. Police, teachers, firefighters, pastors, hospital workers, social workers, school administrators, and counselors of any kind are among those squarely in the target area. Those who study the issue are quick to point out that it primarily comes from a lack of reward rather than overwork. Here is a list that will help you determine whether or not you have burnout or the early symptoms of depression.

1. Watching too much television
2. Little interest in sex
3. Self-depreciating humor
4. Lack of physical exercise
5. Dark thoughts, even of suicide; a sense of being trapped; hopelessness

6. Overeating
7. Too much coffee or alcohol
8. Excessive anger, short-fused
9. Nothing will please
10. Inability to sleep
11. Cynicism and the loss of idealism
12. Self-depletion; output exceeds input

The term *burnout* first came into popular use with the publication of Herbert Freudenberger's book *Burnout*.[3] Dr. Freudenberger defined burnout as "A state of fatigue or frustration brought about by devotion to a cause, way of life, or relationship that failed to produce the expected reward." He gave some definite ways to overcome it, which we will discuss later. Pastors and other church workers generally resist acknowledging that they are depressed, or "burned out." After all, we think we are above such human difficulties.

There *is* a road back from burnout city, and we all must take it if we are to have a healthy life and productive ministry. Let us first look at the need for all of us to examine ourselves and determine what we are communicating to our people. We communicate our personal situation to the people around us long before we acknowledge it to ourselves. We cannot *not* communicate.

When we walk into a room, people begin to size us up immediately—our projection of self-image, the level of our self-care, and our enthusiasm or lack of it.[4] Theorists claim that only fifteen percent of what we communicate is verbal. The rest is nonverbal. Our body language, facial expressions, posture, eyes, voice tone, speed or slowness of speech, and how we are dressed tell the other eighty-five percent.

A stressed-out pastor cannot give witness to the Good News and the wholesome Christian life. Regardless of whether or not we say the right thing in a sermon or beside a hospital bed, the nonverbal will prevail. When we are burned out, we are usually dull, hollow, pessimistic, uninteresting, and have little excitement about us.

Self-care is not destructive self-indulgence, but rather it is being a steward of some rather special gifts—the human body and soul, along with the capacity to bring joy to others as well as to experience it. Charles Spurgeon observed that the farmer is working just as hard when he is sharpening his plow as when he is tilling the soil with it. The fisherman is working as hard when he mends his nets as when he casts them. It is a commitment we make to God when we accept His call to serve. It takes courage to take care of yourself. One of the hallmarks of a professional is the ability to keep healthy—physically, emotionally, and spiritually. You must take responsibility for yourself and not expect others to take the initiative to care for you.

Many of us enjoy being a victim, and being a victim of the ministry is the best of all worlds. We're a victim of the deacons, our predecessor's mistakes, a family that doesn't understand, and on it goes. Once the victim status is established, we can then sit around waiting for someone to rescue us, and we become terribly upset with those we think should rescue us because they do not come quickly enough.

Here are some of the things Carolyn and I decided to do. They may not be radical, but, hopefully, they will give others courage to think through their own personal disciplines. These coping mechanisms came about in our lives because we needed then for survival. Because of them, we have been able to stay in this work longer than we ever imagined we could.

SABBATH TIME: Nowhere do we read in the Bible that the tribe of Levi was not to find time to worship. The Sabbath was for *all* of God's people, including those who served in the

Temple. It is a unique gift that is little appreciated, but may be one of the reasons the Jews have survived so long and so well. Carolyn and I decided we deserved a Sabbath too, and Sunday could not be that day. Just like a football coach, Sunday is game day. Our role is to help the church to have meaningful worship and to proclaim and teach the Gospel. This takes from us; we are the feeders of the people, not the fed. A pastor cannot feed the church out of an empty heart.

There is much written now on the Sabbath. It seems that it has been rediscovered by the Christian community in recent years. In fact, Christian writers writing about the Sabbath seems to be a cottage industry. No longer is it seen as a bunch of "blue laws" contrived to take the fun out of life once a week. Sabbath is truly a gift from God. It was made for us, not we for it. "Six days you shall labor and do all your work, but the seventh day is a Sabbath to the Lord your God" (Exodus 20:8–10). This is metaphor for how God has provided for us to keep body and soul together. We are to be mindful of our souls. God has called us to set aside a timeless time for catching our breath and savoring life. We cannot make meaning simply by willing it; we must make space for it by allowing for the working of the unconscious activity of the soul. In *Minding the Soul*, James B. Ashbrook writes an important section on Sabbath.[5] This has been helpful to my deeper understanding of this concept.

Carolyn and I vowed to take a weekly Sabbath. This is not a day off to wash the car or run errands. Neither is it a day to catch up on office work nor to make that visit that must be made before Sunday. This is a day of personal worship and meditation in addition to the private devotions and prayer we conduct the other six days. For us, the best day for this is after Wednesday and before Sunday. When our children were at home, we would get them off to school and then spend some time together quietly reading and talking about what we had read, praying silently and together. We would also tell each other our hopes, dreams, fears, and, when the weather permitted, we would take a walk, together or separately, and usually have a very simple meal. The afternoon is usually filled with light recreation and/or reading. The evening for us has been a time of ending the Sabbath and celebrating. Always make space to celebrate. Celebration is as important as mourning. In fact, when you and your spouse are looking for things to celebrate, your thinking about the difficult things is changed.

While in seminary, it was highly recommended and generally accepted that the minister would spend the mornings in the study exegeting Greek verbs or reading heavy theology and preparing sermons. The afternoon was spent visiting shut-ins and doing the usual church administration, while the evening was spent with the family, helping the children with their homework as the wife played the piano in the background. Not only was this unrealistic for us, it was also grossly out of touch with the realities of parish life, or any other kind of life for that matter.

For us, the week divides differently than I expected in preparation for the pastorate. Sunday through Wednesday are public times for me, consumed with worship, committee meetings, counseling, staff meetings, working with laymen, and service outside of the church. Thursday through Saturday is my quiet time. It is during this time that I celebrate a Sabbath, study, write, take some time off, and do the heavy lifting of sermon preparation. The whole discipline of sermon preparation will be covered in another chapter.

REGULAR AND VIGOROUS EXERCISE: Exercise does not come easy to me, but I have found that I work much better, feel better, and manage my weight better if I have an exercise routine. In the early days of ministry, I exercised at a health club or at the YMCA. Now I have the basics (treadmill, free weights, etc.) in my study at home, and there is no way to get away from it. Usually Carolyn and I have a light breakfast and go to the health room three or four days a week before we start our day. It is not unusual for us to do a very light workout early on Sunday morning. This makes certain that I don't show up at church with low energy levels. Who wants to hear a sluggish preacher?

A national publication reports that a recent survey found that CEOs of major companies all exercised regularly.[6] Their vigorous routines lasted from thirty to sixty minutes a day. Leaders keep themselves in shape.

Even though I'm not a Jack LaLanne or Charles Atlas, I am convinced that exercise is one of the things that has made a significant difference in our lives. Carolyn and I have had no serious illnesses and still have the energy to serve well past retirement age. In a health-conscience world, it seems counter-productive to ask your people to listen to you tell them about the good life while your very demeanor shows a life of indulgence and neglect of the basic health rules.

DEVELOP A SUPPORT NETWORK: This is extremely diffi-cult for the parish minister to accomplish without compromising his leadership in the church. There are a host of people in every church who are ready to be our best friends, and we know instinctively that their motives are not that genuine. They may wish to influence our preaching or the direction of the church's ministry. They may have other motives that would cripple our ministries beyond repair.

When I started serving in Atlanta many years ago, I was young and so was the church. One evening at a dinner party (made up mostly of other young adults), several of the young men took me aside and suggested that we form an alliance. They would help me lead the church, and we could replace the current leadership. After all, we were the same age. In their minds, the current leadership was old and out-of-date. I refused their offer. I politely told them that I had been called to serve the entire church, not just one age group, and I hoped they would understand. They really didn't, and they were never comfortable with my leadership the entire time I was at that church.

In an ideal world it would be nice to have strong friends outside the church and from another denomination, if possible. From time to time, we have had this. We have found, though, that laymen, however committed to the church, are never really able to let you take off your uniform or step out of your role and just be friends with them. However you slice it, the clergy thing is still there. Their advice is still given on theology, church procedure, or, God forbid, politics.

One day I received a call from a pastor in another denomination in another city who was anxious to talk to me about a problem in his church. When he came to talk, he was very distressed. It seems that he and his wife were very good friends with a group of couples in his church who spent holidays together and enjoyed social evenings together almost every week. This pastor and his wife enjoyed it and found that their group was very supportive of his ministry until the church had to make some difficult decisions about its future direction. He was upset because they no longer included him and his wife in their social plans. The group had a different vision for the future of the church than he did as pastor. He felt like an outcast and was not sure if he could stay there much longer if his worst fears were true. He asked me, "What should I do?" I assured him that I thought he could continue in his position and that he was acting out of fear. However, I thought that he and his wife should rejoice that he had been dropped by the group. Now that they were no longer captive to a small social group within the church, they could find friends outside the church or new friends inside the church if they wanted to take that risk again. He had never thought of it that way. We all need friends, but they are so hard to find. It is also hard to serve the entire church because there are some people you like better than others, yet you are the pastor of the whole church.

Some would suggest that other clergy would be the ideal friends for a pastor and his family. In some situations this is correct. However, the jealousy factor comes into play in some cases. Many clergy have been able to get past this and have formed strong bonds with other clergy. I have found this is best when the age difference is pronounced. Older and younger clergy are not as competitive as clergy of the same age. The best clergy relationships I have had have been with clergy of other denominations. The competition factor is almost gone, and the learning experience is always fruitful when we are together.

Dr. Frank Harrington, the longtime pastor of the Peachtree Road Presbyterian church in Atlanta, and I had a very special relationship. Our churches were in the same neighborhood, and we worked together on many community and interfaith projects. It so happened that my home was midway between his church and his house. One Monday night I heard a knock at our door and was surprised to find Frank there. I invited him in, and we had a wonderful time talking together. This occurred about once a month at the same time on Monday nights. From this tradition developed a strong friendship. What I later figured out was that Frank was coming by the house after the meeting of his official board, and we provided a place for him to debrief before he got home.

Frank and I traveled together, attending several preaching programs in the United States and England. We even hosted some church-growth events together. When I left the Wieuca Road Baptist Church, Frank came by my house as usual on a Monday night and suggested that if I were open to it, he could help me find a pulpit in the Presbyterian church. I thanked him for this gracious act, but I was soon to be called to the First Baptist Church of Chamblee, Georgia. I knew my way around the Baptist world and our problems, but I was not sure of how to deal with Presbyterian problems. Frank died a few years later. The men of his church took turns sitting by his bed around the clock at the hospital, and I was honored to take my turn with my dear friend.

LEARN TO LAUGH AGAIN: Dealing with very serious issues day after day can be a joy-killer. Humor has been easy for me from the beginning of my ministry. In my mind, there are two ways that humor is used by speakers. One is the speaker who just tells one joke after another. Bob Hope and Jay Leno are good examples of this. They are funny, command large audiences, and are very effective. The other kind of comedian has humor that flows up out of his personality, and, for the most part, his wit cannot be manufactured or easily controlled. It seems to come from a deeper place within. I think Robin Williams is an example of the latter type of comedian. I have more in common with the former rather than the latter comedian. Humor had always been a release for me, and it came quite naturally. During college and seminary I made some spending money by entertaining at church banquets. Later I did a lot of work on the motivational circuit using the gift of humor. Early in my ministry I found that humor could, if used properly, defuse a difficult situation in a committee meeting or make a point in a sermon. It is a very healthy and effective tool. It can also provide comic relief in a sermon.

One evening after church during my first year in Atlanta, a very dour deacon took me aside and gave me this warning: "Young man," he said, "you'll never make it in Atlanta until you lose that humor!" I was devastated and spent some time thinking and praying about it. What should I do with this gift? I truly thought it was a gift. For several weeks I tried to suppress it. Without the spark of a natural flow of humor, my sermons were flat and quite depressing. The congregation noticed it, and some were courageous enough to mention it to me. I made this a matter of prayer as well as study. The conclusion for me, and it came during a long session of prayer, was that God had made me this way; this was a unique gift and should be used. I needed to set boundaries around it and discipline myself in using it. I determined that I should never use it to hurt anyone or any group, nor should it be used as a substitute for study, prayer, and the general hard work of the ministry. It was helpful when I discovered that I was able take the Gospel very seriously but not take myself very seriously at all. I think this distinction is crucial.

During this period I became aware of the work of Norman Cousins, the retired editor of *The Saturday Review*. He did considerable work in what he called "laughter therapy." The details of this can be found in his book.[7] Here, he traces his struggle with a blood disease that the medical profession had difficulty treating. He discovered that after he had enjoyed a session of laughter with friends, his blood sedimentation rate improved. Alan Funt, the producer of the television program "Candid Camera," sent over some of the funniest of his classic programs. Cousins called his family together, and they enjoyed them enormously. They made the joyous discovery that ten minutes of genuine belly laughter had an anesthetic effect that would give him at least two hours of pain-free sleep. After this discovery, he checked out of the hospital and moved into a hotel, requiring everyone who came into the room to tell him a joke or a funny story. He and his family would watch reruns of old movies and TV comedies. This, along with the enlightened cooperation of his doctors, helped him through this difficult time. Cousins recovered enough to go back to his work at *The*

*Saturday Review* full time. That in itself was a miracle. He spent his last years teaching laughter therapy to doctors at the UCLA School of Medicine. His book, *Head First*[8] is a chronicle of his work there.

Carolyn and I determined that we have a life, even if those around us did not want to have a life or want us to have one, and that nothing in the church, its people, or its organization was going to keep us from having a life—a healthy, full, and enjoyable life—and to laugh a lot. We took our Sabbath, even when very powerful families demanded attention. We spent time with our children and ourselves, even when minor church activities would claim our time. We traveled in spite of the fact that critical people suggested that we should stay home. "After all, there are a lot of people in the church that cannot travel," they said.

Incidentally, the pastor's extended family can be a deterrent to the effort to have a full and meaningful life as well. Many pastors have shared with me that their siblings or other members of their extended family have brought unusual pressure on them to spend an inordinate amount of time taking care of them. "What good is it to have a pastor in the family if you can't get some extra care from him?"

There comes a time when the pastor and spouse must decide again that "in order to care of them best I must cater to them less." To do this, it is important to laugh, enjoy each other, step out of uniform, and give your serious side a rest. Laughter *is* the best medicine. "Laughter helps us transcend our suffering, crying does not."[9]

DO NOT BE AFRAID OF THERAPY: The minister constantly deals with highly emotional problems in a highly volatile arena. It is important to have a professional available to talk to on a regular basis. Not one of us is sufficient unto ourselves to deal with the situations we face alone. The whole matter of counseling is a unique subject. I have found that I am able to handle most problems that I am called on to deal with only on an emergency basis. Most clergy have had the basics of counseling courses in seminary, but none of us is capable of taking on the responsibility of deeper work with our people. I have decided that I am like an emergency room at the hospital. I can stop the bleeding, but after that I send them on to a therapist who can be trusted to deal with their issues at a much deeper level than I can. In fact, most church members do not want their pastor to know that much about them. After all, he does preach to the group every Sunday, and they may end up as a sermon illustration. Nor do they want to be reminded of this every time they go to church. Many times, those who come to me for counseling move to another church, simply because they are embarrassed to have their secrets known by the pastor, even though all was done in strictest confidence. Every church member lives in fear of being a sermon illustration.

In order to protect all involved and to ensure that they receive the best help, I have developed a group of pastoral counselors for referral who are able to go the distance with my people. I have found that people receive the counseling better if I prepare them for what they might experience, because most individuals are frightened by the idea of seeing someone. I assure them that the counselor is not trying to destroy them emotionally, and that it may take several sessions to notice any difference. If they do not feel comfortable with the counselor, they are not required to continue the sessions. If they wish to discontinue the sessions because they do not feel that there is a good fit with the counselor, it doesn't mean that counseling is bad, but rather that the relationship did not work. On more than one occasion, I have helped people find other counselors who were a better fit.

That said, I have also decided that I need an emotional check-up on a regular basis from a trusted friend and competent counselor. This has been highly valuable to me. On occasion, Carolyn attends these sessions with me. Through the years this has made a great difference in our ministry. It has made me more sensitive to the needs of people and more understanding of my own feelings. When I share this with the people I am sending to a counselor, they are much more willing to go themselves. I have never understood why we as a culture are so afraid of getting help with our feelings. No competent counselor will destroy the structure that holds a person together. Find someone to refer your people to and find someone to go to yourself.

# 6

NOW ABIDETH ADMINISTRATION,
COUNSELING, AND PREACHING,
BUT THE GREATEST OF THESE IS PREACHING:
THE IMPORTANCE AND POWER OF PREACHING
HOW TO FIND YOUR OWN VOICE

"The church is dead." This has been the cry of every decade since I have been in the ministry. In fact, it seems as though no respectable clergy could write a book about the ministry without an angry denunciation of the church. Most books written about the church that I have read during my ministry are either written by an angry pastor who has left the pastorate or an academic who has little firsthand experience as a pastor. One exception to this is a book by Helmut Thielicke entitled *The Trouble with the Church.*[10] Thielicke places the blame for the inadequacy of the church squarely on the pulpit. He contends that the church is dead where the pulpit is dead, and the church is alive where the pulpit is alive.

Why are our pulpits dead? If our pulpits are dead, there are several reasons for it. First of all is the scorn and contempt that many preachers have for the task of preaching. Donald Miller, in his book *The Way to Biblical Preaching*, says: "If Protestantism ever dies with a dagger in its back, the dagger will be the Protestant sermon." A candidate for the ministry once remarked to me, "I consider preaching to be a necessary evil. I shall do as much as demanded by my position so that I may do other things closer to my heart. I wish to avoid it altogether." Several young men and women have noted to me that they want to preach but not every week. It is now fashionable among seminarians to say "I'm not an every-Sunday preacher."

There is a loss of confidence in the effectiveness of preaching. Many good pastors preach routine sermons expecting and receiving only a few positive results. Recently I talked with a group of clergy and asked them what they considered to be the role of preaching in the life of the church. All of them responded that they had little confidence in the effectiveness of preaching for building the church.

In an attempt to attract a hearing, some ministers have presided over a combination of a religious circus and vaudeville show, booking every visiting religious singing group, public speaker, or advocate coming through town, hoping that this somehow will enliven their churches. This may tantalize for a day, but it certainly does not build any long-term relationships within the church.

Others have used the format of a rock concert with a motivational speech masquerading as a sermon added to it. Some have called these "7-11 services": they sing seven words for eleven minutes.

Other pastors, in a desperate effort to prove to themselves and to the world that they are significant and worthy people, have tried to justify their existence by showing how active they can be in the church, denomination, and community. This is not a plea for the pastor to be invisible six days a week and incomprehensible on the seventh. It is a recognition that everything on the pastor's calendar from Monday to Saturday takes away from time studying, praying, and preparing to bring the word of God to God's people.

The pulpit is the last place in our culture where a person

stands before essentially the same group of people each week and opens his heart to them. I know of no other place where this audience is inclusive in age, education, social position, experience (both religious and personal), and who are there because of their free choice. Other audiences, such as schools, business groups, or civic clubs, are easier to maintain because they have attendance requirements, are composed of members who are usually of the same age, and are focused on clearly defined goals. The speaker is dispensing information and is not primarily trying to establish a long-term relationship that would change their lives by relating them to God in a religious experience.

It is reported that when Winston Churchill left office after World War II, it was suggested that he become a preacher. After all, he possessed gifts of speaking and writing. Churchill replied, "I am not such a fool as to think that I could speak to essentially the same people about the same subject each week and keep their attention." Every pastor faces that challenge each week.

The confusion of ministerial roles has also contributed to a decline in preaching. Samuel Blizzard asked 1,300 ministers to arrange six role functions in the order of their importance. Seven hundred replies gave this order: preacher, pastor, priest, teacher, organizer, and administrator. But when the roles were arranged in order of time actually spent, they came out administrator, pastor, priest, organizer, preacher, and teacher. The ministers said that preaching was primary, but they practiced it at the fifth level.[11]

Church people also confuse the ministerial role. Many times they talk about wanting effective pulpit work and a significant worship encounter. However, they play an effective game of demanding personal services and asking that the minister jump to their tune. Yet the people cannot have a clear vision of the role of the minister until the pastor settles his own mind about it.

Laziness is a temptation for all clergy. It is easier to visit than to organize. It is easier to attend a committee meeting and to become a community functionary than it is to struggle with a passage of scripture, wrestle with an idea, spend time in prayer (sometime prayer is a struggle), and think a sermon through. Since the pastor does not punch a time clock every morning and evening, it is easy to find places to hide and to be lazy. This has been done by some pastors.

Occasionally I hear a pastor complain that there is not any freedom in the pulpit. It has been my experience that the people will let the pastor have as much freedom as the pastor will claim for himself, and that the pulpit is stronger and the church is freer when the pastor takes this freedom. If the pastor has paid his dues by showing his love and care of the congregation, they will be understanding at this point. I have also noticed that churches give the pastor an "eccentricity quotient," which allows him to be a little different on certain issues.

What is preaching anyway? Before we can deal with this positively, we may have to look at some negative ideas about preaching. First of all, preaching is not just "religious talk" in which one person gives his views on theological, psychological, sociological, and philosophical subjects, nor is it public speaking with a religious flavor which degenerates into some talk about God. Some have said that preaching is only specialized public speaking, but all of these definitions fall short.

There are some definitions that have stood the test of time. Phillips Brooks has said "preaching is the communication of truth by man to men; preaching is the bringing of truth through personality."[12] Henry Sloan Coffin reminds us that, "preaching is truth through a personality to constrain conscience at once."[13]

What is preaching? Preaching is God talking. God is not so much the object as the source of Christian preaching. Thus, preaching is speech by God rather than speech about God. When preaching is understood this way, it becomes a very heavy responsibility. The preacher carries God's word to the people. The preacher is God's ambassador; God is entreating through the preacher. In true preaching, the preacher does more than just speak about the mighty acts of God for human salvation. He preaches in order that God may say these things Himself.

Ideally, preaching is an event in which God acts. It is an event in the life of the community in which the dynamic of the biblical event is recreated in the worship encounter and the people live through it again. P. T. Forsyth was adamant when he declared that preaching is "the Gospel prolonging and declaring itself."[14] True preaching is an event that effectively communicates the power and redemptive activity of God. When the redemptive acts of God in Christ are proclaimed, Christ is present to act redemptively.

Preaching is "the word of God which He Himself has spoken," says Karl Barth. "But he makes use, according to His good pleasure, of the ministry of a man who speaks to his fellowmen, in God's name, by means of a passage of scripture. Such a man fulfills the vocation to which the church has called him, and through his ministry, the church is obedient to the mission entrusted to her."[15] I would also agree with Martin Luther, who said, "The preaching of the word of God is the Word of God."[16]

We have a good example of this in the ministry of Jesus. Although Jesus was healer, counselor, and teacher, He obviously gave preaching a central place in his ministry. The Gospel writers continually affirm that Jesus came preaching. He declared that He was anointed by God to "preach the Gospel to the poor ... to preach deliverance to the captives ... to preach the acceptable year of the Lord" (Luke 4:18–19). "I must preach the good news of the Kingdom of God ... for I was sent for this purpose" (Luke 9:6). Let us remember that Jesus sent His disciples through the villages preaching the Gospel. When the pastor stands to preach, the pastor is in the tradition of the prophets, the company of the apostles, and the fellowship of Jesus, who came preaching the Gospel. In Mark 1:38, He said, "Let us go into the next towns, that I may preach there also; for therefore came I forth."

The emphasis of the church through the years has been on preaching. Prophecy and oratory preceded Christian preaching, but the preacher came into his own with Christianity. Preaching is specifically Christian. The early church made preaching central. "How shall they hear without a preacher?" (Romans 10:14). "Preach the word, be urgent in season and out of season, convince, rebuke, and exhort, be unfailing in patience and in teaching" (2 Timothy 4:2). "But hath in due times manifested his word through preaching, which is committed unto me according to the commandments of God our Savior" (Titus 1:3).

I agree with the great Paul Scherer, who said, "There is not now nor has there ever been an acceptable substitute for Christian preaching."[17] It is a bold statement, but it must be said: with its preaching, Christianity stands or falls. In the last three decades we have started to fall because our pulpits have stumbled and fallen. I believe that we are not all destined to be great preachers, but we can all be better preachers.

Several years ago, I was invited by the Home Mission Board (now called the North American Mission Board) of the Southern Baptist Convention to preach for a week at their summer emphasis on the Baptist assembly grounds at Ridgecrest, North Carolina. The major feature of the week was the worship each night, and the preacher carried a heavy responsibility for the success of the week. A few days before the assembly was to begin, I received word from the board that the program had been changed, and instead of having a preacher they were going to have panel discussions, skits, and other short dramatic presentations. I agreed to the change. It gave me my time back and I could use it to be with my family. About two days into the week, though, I received a call from Ridgecrest, asking me if I could come and rescue the week. The administrator who called apologized for the situation. It seems that a group of young leaders inside the board had decided that preaching was not effective and had insisted that this new program format would fill the 2,000-seat meeting hall each night. But it had not worked. Very few people were attending the evening sessions, and the week was falling apart. "What we need is a preacher, and I have been asked to see if you would come and rescue the week for us." He apologized profusely for the situation and pled with me to come to Ridgecrest and finish out the week for them. I did, and the week was a Pentecost. There was a movement of the Holy Spirit among the people and this preacher as well. When will we learn that God's people are led, fed, and empowered by the "foolishness of preaching"?

Pastor, never, never, never let anyone steal from you God's claim on your tongue as preacher. Never forget that there will come a day when we shall stand before the great white throne and from it there shall sound a voice like unto that of the Son of God, asking, "I gave you my Gospel; what did you do with it?" I contend that our people have not grown tired of the Gospel, but rather they have rarely heard it. They have grown weary of the words of truth being filtered through movies and novels. They are hungry to hear the word of God from a preacher appointed by God who has paid the price of preparation and whose heart is aflame with a fire from heaven. Charles Spurgeon said it best:

> If there be a place under high heaven more holy than another, it is the pulpit whence the gospel is preached. This is the Thermopylae of Christendom; here must the great battle be fought between Christ's church and the invading host of a wicked world. This is the last vestige of anything sacred that

is left to us. We have no altars now; Christ is our altar. But we have the pulpit still left, a place which, when a man entereth, he might put off his shoes from his feet, for the place whereon he standeth is holy. Consecrated by the Savior's presence, established by the clearness of the force of apostle's eloquence, maintained and upheld by the faithfulness and fervor of a succession of evangelists who, like stars, have marked the era in which they lived and stamped with their names, the pulpit is handed down to those of us who occupy it now with the prestige of everything that is great and holy.[18]

There is a sign in my study displayed so that I can see it as I prepare sermons. It is a variation of a sign displayed in Bill Clinton's campaign office in Little Rock, Arkansas, during his first run for the presidency. Clinton's sign read, "*It's the economy, stupid.*" My sign reads, "*It's communication, stupid.* "It reminds me that my people are not as interested in getting to heaven as they are in getting to Friday. They are not primarily interested in the distance from Jerusalem to Jericho as they are in how to live their lives in a very threatening world. In order to be in church on Sunday, or any other day, they have decided against doing any of five other things that are important for their lives. Their children are pulled in many other directions every weekend to events that are exciting, well prepared, and well promoted. There must be instant communication with their needs, as well as their wants. Because of their various situations, they want to know the time of day, not how to build a clock. There is no respect for Sunday as sacred space on the community calendar as in former days. Well-meaning secular charities, school programs, school athletic practices, and games are scheduled on Sundays. The county in which I serve has a soccer program with over 500 participants every Sunday morning about one mile from our church.

Compounding this is a sense of hopelessness and quiet

desperation on the part of many sensitive families. Our best neighborhoods have their fatherless homes, where father travels all week and is home only on weekends. We also have our displaced persons, as corporations move their people around every few years creating corporate migrants. They lose their sense of community. This quiet desperation can be as damaging as any inner-city situation. The families broken by divorce abound. Drugs and alcohol proliferate in middle-class America as they do in the ghetto.

In the face of this, the question for the preacher is *how can we communicate anything to anyone in an age like this?* The old clichés do not seem to hold any meaning. Words like grace, repentance, and salvation seem empty in the light of alienation, loneliness, and hopelessness.

Like most preachers trained in the traditional methods of ministry, this situation was amplified in that I was ministering to a highly educated congregation that would not be stampeded by promotional gimmicks or manipulated by an ecclesiastical con man. Most of us have been educated to minister in a county-seat town with one hospital and a merchants' association that encouraged every store to close on Wednesday afternoon and all day Sunday. The minister in this situation was a cross between the local congressman, who must always keep his fences mended in order to be reelected, and a puppet, easily manipulated by carping, whining, and strategically placed gossip. His reward for properly feeling the pulse of the community often was a new automobile on his tenth anniversary or a trip to the Holy Land. In large metropolitan areas, it is impossible to shake enough hands often enough to make a significant difference. The choices in priorities are between ministering to a broken family or a broken life rather than visiting the "right" people or playing golf with influential individuals. The old methods of ministry are impossible. The old words have little meaning, and the old styles of ministry have little connection with this culture.

I mentioned that we minister to a highly educated population, and that is true. But the education is, in some ways, so specialized that it is only training to do a specific task, work a machine, repair equipment, sell a product, or organize a sales group. It is not education in the broadest sense, that which enables a person to wrestle with ideas and come to some conclusion of his own. When this is brought into church and the preacher asks the congregation to consider an idea from several angles, it is all but impossible for them to do so. In most cases, instead of wrestling with the text or a doctrine, many people just want their activities and ideas confirmed and their opinions, which have been shaped by the harsh rhetoric of talk radio, justified. People, like water, usually take the path of least resistance.

Communicating in this situation is even more frustrating. The old methods of sermon preparation—squeezing the Greek verbs until they hurt and setting up propositions (usually three) that resulted from this process and giving this to the congergation—are not meeting their needs. Many preachers live in fear that their old seminary professor will attend a service unannounced, and that they will be caught with their propositions down.

In my pilgrimage in this traditional situation, I noticed that when all of the traditional structure for communicating from the pulpit was abandoned and I openly shared myself and the scripture with the congregation (regardless of whether or not the invisible professor was present), something would begin to happen. This does not eliminate the need for structure in the sermon. I have come to believe that the structure in a sermon is like the bones in the human body. If you see the bones, the body is in trouble. However, you should be able see the evidence of the bones being there. Some preachers make the framework of their sermons very clear to the listener. Their points are evident and clearly numbered ... point one, point two, point three. This reminds me of a medieval cathedral with the flying buttresses on the outside of the building holding up the walls. Other preachers, usually younger ones, do not make the structure of their sermons so evident. This is like buildings constructed after engineers developed ways of putting the support within the walls. Both ways accomplish their purpose. Both methods of sermon construction are useful.

I could not leave this section without some word about sermon preparation. There is not just one and only one way to prepare. Each pastor has developed a method that fits his personality and needs. I will walk through my system (not that it is perfect) since it has been hammered out through trial and error throughout the years and it fits my needs. It is still a work in progress.

I am a very verbal person and find that I work best from what is called an "oral manuscript." I have been doing this all of my ministry. In the early years, I felt very guilty about this, because in school the preacher who read a manuscript (ready for publication) to his church on Sunday was always considered to be the ideal. It was not until I read Clyde Fant's book, *Preaching for Today* (Harper & Row, 1975), that I developed an element of peace about this. He talks about the "oral manuscript." It is researched, rehearsed, organized, and well developed but not primarily delivered from a written manuscript. In my case, I use a very detailed outline, primarily because I am so verbal that I need the outline to keep me from chasing every rabbit that comes across my path. I talked to Clyde about this and told him that I wish that I had been able to get this into print before he did. However, I was grateful to him for giving the "oral manuscript" a name, and making it legitimate.

Early in the summer each year, I take several boxes of books and a church calendar to a cottage in the North Carolina mountains for about three weeks to plan my preaching for the next year. (I have done this in only one week.) Most of the time I plan for the nine months of the school year and leave the summer months for miscellaneous things that I have wanted to say during the year and for some reason could not. After much prayer and reading, a theme and direction begin to form. When I am satisfied that this is the way God is leading, I write the plan down and send it to my ministry assistant. It is published in the church paper and on our website and is used as a guide for the planning of worship. Some years I have only planned through Advent and Christmas, then announce a January through May plan during the Christmas season. This creates renewed interest in the pulpit. The plan is usually broken into month-long segments that support the general theme for the year.

Some pastors use the lectionary as their preaching guide. This is commendable. I have found it helpful, especially during the Christmas and Easter seasons. I do agree with those who use it that it forces the preacher to deal with texts that would ordinarily be avoided because of their difficulty. Baptist seminaries did not teach us to use the lectionary when I was a student, and so my habits were formed early not to use it. Today, many Baptist seminaries are including the lectionary as a part of the curriculum; this is an improvement.

The planning on my part has been well received by the congregation as well as the staff, as it lets the church know that there is some focus and movement in the pulpit. I don't just think up something to say on Saturday night. If I take preaching seriously, they will take it seriously. I have been in homes and have seen my list of sermons posted on the family refrigerator. Some people keep the list in their Bibles to guide their reading during the week. Naturally, the plan can be adjusted as needed through the year. An example was the tragedy of the destruction of the World Trade Center on September 11, 2001. When this occurred, I was in a series of sermons on the Ten Commandments. I immediately adjusted what I was preaching to meet the challenge of that period in our national history and to help our people deal with it.

As I have mentioned earlier, my week is divided into two parts. Sunday morning through Wednesday night is the public time. Committee meetings, involvement with the staff, as well a community organizations, counseling, and outreach assignments are scheduled for that part of the week. Thursday morning through Saturday night is my quiet time. Sometime during that period I take a Sabbath, relax with my family, and finish up Sunday's sermon. In the best of all worlds, I would have the sermon finished by Friday night and would take Saturday afternoon and evening to prepare myself. An old preacher once said to me that the pastor must read himself full, think himself straight, and pray himself hot. That about covers it. I spend Saturday night praying myself hot. I do not take an engagement on Saturday, except perhaps a wedding, and I limit myself only to the ceremony. I do not attend the reception or other social engagements.

If all has gone well, I can get the sermon in shape to preach by Friday afternoon. From that time on, I spend time preaching the sermon, preparing the "oral manuscript," if you please. There is also the concentrated quiet time on Saturday night when I pray and preach in my study. Then early on Sunday morning I do the same, and again before breakfast with Carolyn. I try to be the first one in the building on Sunday and go directly to the sanctuary and take a seat in the pews, imagining what it would be like to listen to the sermon as a church member or visitor. I also take time to walk around the room and pray for those who will be worshiping that day, by name, if possible. When Sunday is over, the entire process starts over again. As I have said earlier, this is not the only way, but it is my way. Each pastor must create his own pattern for preparation.

One word about the preacher's library: I am a "bookaholic." I think that a pastor cannot have too much material at his disposal. I have an extensive library at my home in my study that is catalogued and cross-referenced. My ministry assistant spends a portion of her time in it each week, keeping it organized and current. However, I do my own research and writing. When inspiration strikes, the preacher must be prepared to take advantage of it. When a reference is needed, no minister has the time to chase down a book somewhere in town. I believe it is better to have it on hand for immediate use. I admit that I'm not as comfortable doing research on the Internet as the younger generation, but I do not discourage it in any way; it's just not my way. For me, there is something magical about holding the book, underlining passages, and even carrying it around. I saw a sign in a store one day that said, "You can't do business out of an empty wagon." I believe that you can't preach out of an empty head or heart! Therefore, I try to have an abundance of resources available when needed. I have always encouraged churches to give their pastor a book and conference allowance. If they want good preaching, they must make some sacrifices too. Churches must be reminded that if they want good preaching, they must provide the encouragement, resources, and the time for the pastor to prepare.

There was a time when I was not in the active pastorate. This lasted for about seven months. I did not use my library as much during that time. Late one evening, I was in the library, and it seemed that the books began to talk to me. "You don't love us as much as you did at one time," they said. It was a very mysterious moment. I had no answer for them except to resume my reading as before. It was not long before I was preaching and studying again. My study is a sacred place, holy ground for me.

One secret of a long and fruitful ministry is to keep oneself fresh by reading and studying. If we preach to the same people for very long, they know our thought patterns and the way we develop ideas. Disciplined study is one way to keep from going stale. Experimenting with new ways of presenting the message helps us to stay fresh. One does not always have to be exclusively topical, exegetical, inductive, or deductive. Over the span of a year we will be all of the above.

Helmut Thielicke says that many preachers are like the cowbird. The cowbird never builds her own nest; she lays her eggs in another's nest. Some preachers never seek to find their own voice. They are content to be a poor imitation of another, to find a style and copy it. They do not read and study; they exist on CDs of the sermons of other pastors. Of course, we should listen to and read the work of other pastors, but it only feeds our souls as we find our own voice and message. Living on other people's work is a formula for failure at worst and mediocrity at best. Finding your own voice does not come easily or without struggle.

There was a time in which young preachers could hear many different preaching styles on one program, usually sponsored by their denomination. Now we are segregated, not only by theology, but by generations. When programs are held that have a preaching component, the preaching styles, the gender of the preachers, and the generations represented on the platform and theology are all alike. I can remember hearing Carlyle Marney, an erudite liberal by Baptist standards, preach a very prophetic sermon to a room full of country preachers, while on the same program Charles Howard, a traveling evangelist, preached with such passion that it seemed that he took the varnish off of the first three rows of pews. Both sermons were accepted and appreciated. This rarely happens now.

One of my high school teachers advised me to listen to

every speaker I could, whether or not I agreed with him. He told me that I would never know who I was until I had listened and studied widely. Because of his word to me, I have heard such diverse speakers as the famed historian Will Durant and the Zen Buddhist Alan Watts. In following his advice, I have grown in my understanding of who I am and how to communicate. As a preacher searches for his voice, his voice slowly finds him. There is no magic formula for this that I am aware of, apart from prayer and study, trial and error, and a lot of listening.

One further word about preaching. An old pastor had delivered a soul-stirring sermon to a room full of young preachers. When he finished, a young seminarian asked him, "Sir, what style of preaching do you use?" The wise old preacher replied, "Son, I just preach the Gospel; you figure out the style." I believe you have become a preacher who has found his voice when you can say that. Preaching is much like learning to drive an automobile. At first, everything is awkward and difficult. With practice, it becomes second nature to shift gears, to adjust the rear view mirror, to use the turn signals. It is the same with the preacher. With practice, he becomes less concerned with gestures, stance, and style. These things become natural and automatic. He knows he has found his voice when he is more concerned with *what* is said rather than with *how* it is said. When the Living Word becomes incarnate in the living situation, as it is wrapped in the flesh and blood of the sermon and preacher, then the preaching event occurs, and Christ comes to His people in the sermon. When this happens you have all you need; your voice becomes His voice. You have not so much found your voice as your voice has been found and used by Him.

There have been times that the sermon has been taken away from me in the preaching event. It seems that something, or Someone, has taken over. I have at times almost had an out-of-body experience while preaching. In these times I have been watching myself preach as I preached. I cannot explain it. Other preachers who have talked about this — such as Tony Campolo in his book, *How to Be Pentecostal Without Speaking in Tongues*[19] — attribute it to the presence of the Holy Spirit. I agree with them. This does not happen every time I preach. I wish it would. But it does happen at the Holy Spirit's discretion, and when it does, it is satisfying beyond anything else in your life.

## 7

## The Church *Is* Worth the Effort!

While Carolyn and I were in London to participate in the International Congress of Preaching, we were walking near Buckingham Palace and noticed a church; actually, it was the shell of a church building that was being rebuilt. There was nothing standing but the four walls—no windows, doors, or pews. Scaffolding was up on the inside of the walls, and the craftsmen were eating their lunch in the nave.

Around the church was a chain link fence with barbed wire across the top. Near the opening that served as a door was a large sign, and these words were written for all to see: "Danger! Enter at your own risk." Those words were designed to protect the general public from construction accidents. I could not resist thinking of the many church professionals, both clergy and support staff, who had been chewed up by the institutional church and would testify to the truth of that sign.

There is a scene early in Margaret Mitchell's classic novel of the Old South, *Gone with the Wind,* of the barbecue at Twelve Oaks plantation. Many young people were there, dressed in their best party attire, flirting, bragging, and having a genuinely good time. During the barbecue, word came that the "War Between the States" had started. The young men donned their uniforms, mounted their horses, and rode off to fight for the Confederacy. They fully believed the war would soon be over and that they would come home victorious and heroes. Not so!

Four years later they came home wounded, hungry, disillusioned, and defeated. They came home to a South that had been burned and looted; all was gone.

This was much like my experience ten to fifteen years after seminary graduation. My phone started ringing with classmates who had entered church ministry with high energy and strong idealism. They were full of Niebuhr, Barth, Brunner, and Tillich, not to mention Greek and Hebrew. They believed that once they explained these theologians to their churches, all would be right in the Kingdom. They thought that there was nothing in the church or denomination that would not be better once they were in control.

These same young men, now older and wiser, called and told me about their brokenness; of churches that would not do the right thing about the race issue, organizational change, or community involvement; of deacons who were masters of political intrigue; of families who were selfish in their demands; of old men and women who excelled in controlling the church and pastor with gossip and innuendo. They told me of their families being harassed by these same people and of the unfair demands placed upon them. They also recited incidents when the denomination and seminaries had abandoned them. The recurrent refrain was "the church is the only army that shoots its wounded." One pastor lamented that being a Baptist is to be abandoned by the denomination. It's much easier to be a Methodist.

I was in Florida some years later speaking to a Cooperative Baptist Fellowship event. I had looked forward to it because many of my former classmates from Stetson University would be there. They were there all right, but most of them had taken early retirement or were involved in secular employment. Some had experienced health and family problems created by the stress of the pastorate. I left the conference thinking that the church was hard on her leaders. I asked myself, "Is the church worth the effort?" Then I remembered ...

The apostle Paul reminds us that "we have this treasure in earthen jars." We are: (1) hard pressed on every side but not crushed; (2) perplexed but not in despair; (3) persecuted but not abandoned; (4) struck down but not destroyed. "We carry His death so that His life may be revealed in our body" (2 Corinthians 4).

These words may provide help if they are exegeted, but they also may be understood from another perspective. They are words of feeling. Let them roll over you. These are not words of glory but of struggle. This reality did not start with the modern church; it has always been with us. I had to remember that they crucified Jesus; they didn't elect Him chairman of the board. Kingdom work, church work, is tough, demanding, and frustrating. It does have its rewards but it is not for the faint of heart. We are educated to understand and preach the treasure, but in reality we spend most of our time on the earthen vessel.

One reason for this is that all the noise is at the shallow end of the pool. While taking our grandchildren swimming one summer, I noticed that in a crowded pool, all the noise was coming from the shallow end. The deep end was also occupied, but the skilled swimmers were there improving their skills, respectful of others and of the rules that guaranteed everyone a good experience. The shallow end was dominated by young, inexperienced swimmers who made strong demands on the lifeguard by breaking or challenging the rules made for their safety and the safety of the larger groups of swimmers. This is like a church, where the immature Christians, regardless of age, are usually the most demanding and the most manipulative. They are constantly challenging or threatening the authority of the lifeguard and dominating the entire pool.

Let's look at the church as it is. It has difficulty with

leadership. Contrary to the New Testament, the pastor is on the bottom of the religious food chain. Seminary usually suggests this, not explicitly, but implicitly. Without realizing it, most students come away from seminary with the feeling that the *smart* students teach. Professors naturally encourage students who write good papers and think academically. They hope to reproduce themselves. The *dedicated* students are encouraged to become missionaries, because they appear to be gifted for this and are used by the seminary to demonstrate its commitment to the task of missions. This plays well with the larger constituency. The *sympathetic* students become counselors. They take the extra courses and work in the hospitals, jails, and nursing homes. The seminaries encourage this because it is so much a part of what the general public thinks ministry is. The *efficient* students become denominational bureaucrats or do some other work utilizing their sense of order and left-brain efficiency. The difficulty comes with all the students who do not clearly fit the profile of one of those specialties. I have actually heard a seminary administrator say, "All the rest of you can become pastors." This clearly implies that it takes no special skill to pastor a church and that the job is for castoffs.

During the Baptist denominational wars, I was having lunch with several former classmates from seminary who were working for the denomination in middle-management positions. They usually had plenty of advice and criticism for those of us who were pastors. Now their seemingly safe jobs were being threatened by those seeking to take over the Southern Baptist Convention. They were frustrated and frightened. Their necks were on the line. Their jobs were being threatened and their security was at stake. They were caught between being true to their ideals and keeping their jobs. Every person around the table said, "If things don't work out, I can always be a pastor." I was the only pastor at the table, and I could not hold back. "I doubt it. Most of you don't have the skills it takes to be a pastor. If you can't take it when you have a comfortable job, how can you expect to perform ministry with the wind of criticism, intrigue, misunderstanding, and gossip in your face every week?"

The pastorate is the normative profession for the Christian community. All else is only a part of what the pastor does. It takes special gifts to become a pastor (Ephesians 4:11). Several years ago a celebrated seminary professor was called as pastor of a fine church in our area. I wrote him to welcome him to the community and included the line, "Welcome to the ministry." Later, after we had become good friends, he told me that the line had bothered him at first. He entered the pastorate thinking his seminary experience would more than suffice, and it would even be an added value for his ministry. He said until he had to face the challenge every day, he did not realize the special set of skills required to be a pastor. Being a pastor is as specialized as any of the other disciplines that are more recognized.

Like the canary in the mineshaft, the church is the early warning system for our culture. Most pastors were making hospital visits and conducting funerals for young men who had a strange and mysterious disease long before the general public was informed by the media of HIV and AIDS. The struggle over race, Vietnam, fundamentalism, the rise of the Religious Right, the rising divorce rate, and women's leadership all were issues most churches faced before they were ever acknowledged by the general public.

The church, as it exists today, is a place in need of informed leadership. While attending a conference at the McAfee School of Theology at Mercer University in Atlanta, this became very clear to me. The attendees were recent graduates and other young church leaders. They were experiencing their first dose of real disillusionment. They talked about people who refused to change organizationally in order for the church to grow. They complained about the unjust criticism and impossible demands placed on their families and especially their children. This went on for the better part of an hour. Finally, Dean Culpepper asked me to respond. I reminded them that it had been my experience that almost all churches have in their makeup a high number of dysfunctional people. Even though these people make the most noise and are hard to lead, they are God's children, too, and need us. We must seek to lead them toward spiritual health and sharing in the welfare of the church. The veteran pastors in the room quickly agreed, and the young pastors responded as though a door to understanding their churches had been unlocked.

The local parish church has confused goals. A George Barna survey taken among laymen asked the question, "What is the purpose of the church?" The answer was quite revealing. Twenty percent said it was to win the world to Jesus Christ by proclaiming the Gospel. Eighty percent of the laymen said that the role of the church was to take care of the parishioners. The same question asked of clergy yielded the exact opposite answer: twenty percent to take care of the parishioners and eighty percent to win the world to Jesus Christ by proclaiming the Gospel. This may be why the old hymn "Rock of Ages, Cleft for Me" is so popular. The church and the Gospel are a place of protection against the storms of life in the mind of most laymen.

This confusion is further evidenced when churches try to write a mission statement. All the personal agendas come rushing to the surface, and this is the hardest task I have ever asked a church to perform. This confusion also shows up when churches try to describe their expectations for the pastor. In most cases the uniform expectation for the pastor is to "meet my needs now."

I was being interviewed by a pulpit committee for an old

church in a large Southern city. The only question I asked was, "What do you expect from a pastor?" After a long pause, one young lady on the committee said, "I want the pastor to be there for me." After some discussion to clarify her answer, I concluded that my wife and I were not a good fit for that church. No one could realistically meet that requirement.

However, in spite of these issues, I still love the church. I love the church universal, as well as the church local (red brick, white-columned, with deacons smoking in the parking lot). With all of its dysfunction and flesh marks, with all of its confusion and humanity, it is still the best thing God has going for Him in this world. We do have this treasure in earthen vessels.

A close reading of history will show that when God does anything in this world, it is done through the church. For me, it is very personal. My mother was a widow who had moved to Delray Beach, Florida, after my father died. I was six years old when we arrived in Delray, and we did not know anyone. The First Baptist Church was poorly organized, had a choir so bad that we were happy when they didn't sing, and the pastors were good men but not highly educated. It seems that they had not read anything since the original transcripts of the Scopes Trial. It was this church that did one thing well for me. They loved my mother and me and became family for us. It was not from their organization that I received help, but rather from their attention and care.

When I was preparing to leave home for Stetson University, they offered to pay my expenses. I was the first young man to receive the call to ministry from this church, and they wanted to be a part of my education. Incidentally, my mother refused the money. She said it would be good for me to work while in school.

It was from this old church that I learned what people should be like. I saw men and women doing the work of the church in such a way that let me know how adults should act when working together. And I saw how well-meaning adults could disagree on issues, big or small, and still work together in community. Church was more than doctrine and organization; church was, and is, community, God's community. Their major contribution to my life was their care for my mother and me. When I hear or read criticism of the church, I feel as though they are criticizing my parents and extended family. Most of us have a profound personal debt to the church.

There is an old story of Zacchaeus after his conversion. It seems that his habit was to rise early each morning and leave home for a while with a rake and shovel in his hand. "Where are you going?" Mrs. Zacchaeus asked one day as he was leaving.

"Do you remember that old sycamore tree I was in when Jesus found me? Well, I'm going to take care of it. It has been neglected by the city fathers and needs my care. You see, it held me so Jesus could find me."

We must remember that Christ loved the church and gave Himself for it. Most of the New Testament is addressed to churches, not individuals. It is pivotal to God's plan for the world (Ephesians) and is the bride of Christ.

It is easy to get people saved, but it takes a church to keep them saved. Let us not forget that the church was in the ghettos before the current crop of activists—note William Booth and the Salvation Army. The church was into education before the government. Note the large number of universities (Harvard, Yale, Princeton) that were started with the express purpose of educating clergy. The church has been feeding the hungry and providing community while the general culture was debating political agendas and power. It was the church that broke down the Berlin Wall, led the March on Selma, produced Martin Luther King, Jr., the civil rights movement, and it was the church that led the War on Poverty.

The church is a solid oak tree, not a fragile teacup. It has withstood Roman Imperialism, Jewish legalism, pagan optimism, medieval institutionalism, the excesses of the reformers, wars and rumors of wars, youth quake, modern skepticism, Southern provincialism, resurgent fundamentalism, and heresies in each generation that seem never to die. It can withstand anything our generation can throw at it, too.

It has been victimized by unprepared and selfish clergy, tone-deaf musicians, manipulative members, argumentative deacons, demanding denominations, unloving reformers, and greedy politicians. Still, it continues to provide love, affirmation, and community to the fallen in the face of alienation.

Serving through the church is a matter of the call and claims of God on your life. The only way one survives and thrives in the church is to know that God has called you to serve this way, recognizing that the church is the bride of Christ.

Many years ago in Bradenton, Florida, we were building the sanctuary of the West Bradenton Baptist church. Because of some unusual circumstances, we were running out of money to complete the project. We devised a plan to encourage the congregation to give more to the building fund. On a Wednesday night we had a church-wide dinner with an inspirational program inside the half-finished building. The contractor was very uneasy about it, but our church leaders were ready to do anything if it could produce the funds to finish the building. On the night of the dinner, as the people were coming in to the tables laden with food, we discovered that there had been a major miscommunication with the roofing subcontractor. He had a crew still working, and they were pouring some kind of liquid roofing compound on the roof. The activity produced a hole in the roof, and a section of tables was covered with this unsightly and gooey stuff. The people were coming into the dinner, and George Schrieffer, our minister of education, and I were desperately trying to rescue the situation, moving tables and chairs and cleaning the area affected. It was panic time. George turned to me and said, "Bill, we could not do this work if we were not called to it, could we?"

To those who are believers and have given up on the church and to those on the outside who do not understand it, I offer this final word. While taking a short vacation to St. Simons Island on the Georgia coast after a very stressful period of ministry, Carolyn and I had an experience that made it very clear for us. We were tired and in need of rest. Preaching, fund-raising, a building program, and the usual daily responsibility of church leadership had taken its toll on us. We were staying at a small motel on the island and spending our time reading, walking on the beach, and visiting the abundant historical sites on the island.

We had made a reservation for an early dinner one evening and were driving along the marshes on the island made famous by the noted Georgia poet, Sidney Lanier, in his famous poem "The Marshes of Glynn." We passed Christ Church, a picturesque white church located on the north end of the island. There is an oak tree standing in a spot near where Charles Wesley had preached. It bears a marker placed there by the State of Georgia. Carolyn insisted that we stop and look at the church. "I've seen a dozen churches just like this, and besides, I'm hungry and we have a dinner reservation. If we stop, we'll be late." Carolyn insisted, and so we stopped.

As we walked up to the church door, I was like a pouting child being forced to do something he did not want to do. We opened the door and the entire atmosphere changed. The sun was setting, and the evening light was coming through the beautiful stained-glass windows at just the right angle. The colors in the ancient wooden pews were deep and mellow, and the reflection on the antique silver communion service at the altar was stunning. We sat on the front pew for a while in total silence, captivated by the entire experience inside this church. As we drove to the restaurant for dinner, neither of us spoke for several minutes. My attitude had changed and I apologized for the way I had acted. We both concluded from that chance experience that you really cannot understand the church from the outside. To know its real meaning, you must be inside; in fact, it must get inside of you.

And now I say to all of the critics of the church—and there are many—if you do not have a church, where do you assemble people to teach them to live by the highest summoning of the human spirit? What do you read that can be called scripture? How do you sing? How do you celebrate?

The church *is* worth the effort. Be grateful you are called to serve God and His people through the church.

8

## Leadership: What I Learned from a Jewish Delicatessen It All Starts at the Top

When I was at the Wieuca Road Baptist Church, I would sometimes walk across the street to a large shopping center to have lunch at a Jewish delicatessen. The owner and I got to be good friends, and he would reserve a seat for me in the back of the deli near the kitchen. From there, I could be out of sight of the customers and enjoy some privacy. While eating there, I observed the way he related to the diners. He always stood at the door and greeted each one as he or she came in. He introduced people to each other, whether he knew them or not, and he never let anyone leave without his personal touch. I thought many pastors could learn from him. The general atmosphere of the deli was joyous, the food was excellent, and it always felt like a party.

As a pastor, I learned a lot from observing this man. The main thing was that the atmosphere of the organization always reflects the attitude of the leader. There is no other way. When he was not there, the atmosphere was much more subdued. As pastors, we have so many ways to affect the attitude of our churches, many of which we do not use. The church picks up on our attitude from the short informal touch or word in the hall, as well as from the pulpit. These short contacts seal the relationship emotionally as no other contact can. Over time it becomes apparent. In recent years I have taken the time to move through

*atmosphere reflects attitude*

the congregation before the service. This shocked people at first. They were accustomed to seeing the pastor enter the sanctuary with the choir, and speaking to them at the front door after the service. While moving through the congregation before the service, I have been able to meet guests who have arrived early, talk to some about church membership who wanted some questions answered, and speak to any number of people I would not have the opportunity to speak with at other times. Studies have shown that the closer the emotional connection between the preacher and the congregation, the greater the impact of the sermon.

On Sunday morning as the people arrive for Sunday school, I try to be at strategic places in the building to greet them, meet the guests, and talk with those who have some special need and wish a quick word with the pastor. Small talk is very important. Duke McCall taught me this in the "School for Scoundrels." The value of small talk is not in its content, but rather in the attention and emotion exchanged in the conversation. It is purely relationship building, and it also lets the pastor know the mood of the day. Chairman Mao is reputed to have said that revolutions are won at two places: on the battlefield and by controlling the gossip at the village well. I have instructed our staff to make sure we control the gossip in the halls on Sunday.

Relationship-building is only one piece of the pastoral leadership puzzle; there is much more to it. Leadership is essential and not easy. Peter Drucker is often quoted as saying, "The four hardest jobs in America are the president of the United States, a university president, a CEO of a hospital, and a pastor."[20] I believe it! Drucker has noted that a leader is someone who has followers, but performing as a leader, especially in a church, is anything but easy.

Leadership is not a license to force others to knuckle under, but it is a skill to perform, a service to render for the whole group. A leader does not do the work better than anyone else. A leader is someone who can get followers to do the work better than he can. A leader brings out the best in other people, casts the vision, dreams the dream, and causes the followers to dream along with him.

In my mind, there seems to be an ambivalence about leadership in the church. I attended a denominational meeting several years ago that offered several seminars concerning issues facing the local church. I attended one led by a fine layman from my church. Its announced subject had to do with encouraging more lay involvement in the life of the church. I was the only pastor in the room. I was there to give the leader encouragement. He did an outstanding job in conducting the meeting, but he could not prevent the meeting from becoming a clergy-bashing session. The twenty laymen in the room regaled us with stories of how they would not let their pastors take any initiative without getting several layers of approval. They shared ways with each other to prevent the pastor from leading the church. He was to be only an errand boy for the congregation.

After this, the meeting took an unusual turn. They began to complain about how dull the church programming was and how people were not responding. Their churches were dead. "What's wrong with us?" they asked. "No one seems to be interested in joining our church." It never occurred to them that they had made certain that that the church had no leadership. They did not connect the fact that they had a dead church with the fact that they had made sure that the shepherd could not lead. The priesthood of believers was never intended to cause the church to be led from the middle, nor was it meant to unpriest the priest or the one qualified to preach, lead, and cast the vision.

It is my contention that whether or not a church is left, right, or center; contemporary, blended, or traditional; no congregation ever registers progress toward avowed goals without strong leadership at the top. Let us remember that Jesus had a job to do and He got it done. He was in charge of His operation. It was He who directed the starts and stops of that little band. He did not get up in the morning in neutral so that outside forces could push Him around. I do not remember Him ever asking the disciples, "Where should we go?" or "What should we do?"

The good of the order is not served when there is no one in charge. I do not read of the sheep telling the shepherd where to go. The sheep are more comfortable when they are led by a called, competent, educated, well-trained professional, not a para-pastor or well-meaning layman. George Buttrick was asked when he planned to have Layman's Day at Madison Avenue Presbyterian Church. His was reported to have replied: "When you observe Layman's Day at Mt. Sinai Hospital and let me perform surgery." This is not a plea for pastoral tyranny, but rather a plea for vocational decisiveness and assertiveness. More churches are hurt by pastoral default than have ever been hurt by pastoral domination. The sheep will follow the shepherd insofar as they determine that the shepherd is following Christ. The shepherd feeds and leads the flock, and the flock nourishes the world. Leadership from the middle is no leadership at all. Too many pastors believe that they should lead, if they lead at all, not from the balls of their feet but from the back of their heels.

Dr. Larry McSwain, professor of Leadership at the McAfee School of Theology at Mercer University in Atlanta, asked me to join six other pastors in a study he was conducting about leadership among evangelical congregations that were not a part of a connectional church system. These congregations were of various sizes and races located throughout the Atlanta metropolitan area. After we had all taken several surveys and had undergone an intense personal examination of our leadership style, we were called together for a group meeting.

The results were more surprising to Dr. McSwain than to those of us participating. In fact, they were so surprising to him that he confessed to the group that the results demanded that he change his theory of leadership and how he taught it.

Dr. McSwain had assumed that churches were best led by a broad-range effort to gain consensus and then to act upon that consensus. The effort usually consisted of many committees working on parts of the project that would bring a report to the church, and then the church would execute the project after consensus was achieved. He found something entirely opposite in his study. All but one of the churches was led by a small group. In each church, the group had a different name and composition and a different authority, but in every case they worked with the pastor to set the course, struggle with the issues, and communicate to the congregation. One participant had been a student in Dr. McSwain's class on leadership and had been terribly frustrated when he tried to lead his church as he had been taught. Without any counsel from the academic world, he shifted his approach to church leadership to the process that was very much like the approach used by the others in the group. Dr. McSwain was quick to acknowledge that he was required by the results of the study to shift the focus of his class.

We have a distorted understanding of leadership. The conventional wisdom about leadership is that the leader is a cross between a dashing Confederate cavalry general or a pulpit Elvis Presley. Somehow pastors have developed a fear of being too authoritarian, too much of a CEO. "Leadership to what end" is the critical question, not "What style is used?" Stalin, Hitler, and Mao possessed great charisma, but they inflicted as much evil and suffering on humanity as has ever been seen. Effective leadership does not depend on charisma. Note that Dwight Eisenhower, George Marshall, and Harry Truman were outstanding leaders, but they possessed about as much charisma as a dead mackerel. Can you imagine a less charismatic leader than Abe Lincoln, a rough, uncouth backwoodsman?

Actually charisma can be the undoing of leaders. It makes them protective of their charm, inflexible, and sensitive about their image. My wife, Carolyn, has always contended that pastors who are blessed with good looks and charisma will not do the hard work of the ministry or take positions that are unpopular for fear they will lose their looks.

Leadership is, first of all, work, and hard work at that. The primary work of a leader is to think through the general mission of the organization, defining it clearly and visibly. The leader sets goals and priorities. The leader also sets and maintains standards. Of course, there are times when the pastor must compromise; we are not masters of the universe. Nevertheless, the leader's first task is to sound the trumpet clear and loud. He should not give an uncertain sound.

Too many of our churches are struggling to determine who and what they are. When I see this, I know there is an absence of leadership at the top. What is the pulpit for, if not to show direction? "If the trumpet give an uncertain sound, who shall prepare for battle" (1 Corinthians 14:8).

It is always difficult to decide which compromise to make. I have concluded that the best rule is to determine whether or not the compromise is compatible with the mission and goals of the church, or if the compromise leads the church away from its mission and goals.

Don't be afraid that a compromise will keep the church from meeting its goals. If the pastor holds fast to a few fundamental standards in his basic conduct, the church will note it and respect it. However, if standards for him are perceived to be what he can get away with, then he will not have followers but hypocritical time-servers. The consistency of standards in the pastor's life and ministry will help keep the church on track in spite of the compromises that must be made along the way.

The pastor, in giving leadership, must make sure that he sees leadership as a responsibility rather than as rank and privilege. When things go wrong, responsibility is accepted by the pastor, and when things go right, the credit is shared with everyone. Taking responsibility was clearly demonstrated when Harry Truman told the country, "The buck stops here."

The effective pastoral leader is not afraid of a strong support staff or of strong lay leadership. He continually holds up to them the goals and direction for the church. He encourages them and gives them resources. He supports them publicly and privately, taking pride in their accomplishments.

There is a risk as a pastor of not having strong and able people around you, and the pastor must be aware of it. Strong people tend to be ambitious, but the greater risk is to be surrounded by weak and incompetent people. They have their own needs and are skilled at upward delegation to the pastor, blaming everything on someone else.

The pastor must be trusted. The most valuable tool in the pastor's toolbox is trust. Without trust there will be no followers. I learned early in the financial campaign at Rocky Mount that this does not mean the pastor is liked by everyone, nor does it mean that everyone agrees with him. But is does mean that you mean what you say, and that you are a person of integrity, and that fact is crucial. Put simply, trust is built when the congregation sees that the pastor's actions and the pastor's words match. Pastor, to be a leader you are not required to be clever or charismatic, but you are required to be consistent and trustworthy.

I cannot leave the discussion of leadership without mentioning a much overlooked portion of pastoral leadership. The wise pastor realizes that the church has two levels of leadership. One is the formal, elected leadership that is recognized and respected by the congregation. The other level is the informal leadership.

A friend of mine was called to a large church in a major Southern city. In the first few weeks he was there, he called his elected leadership together and shared with them his goals for the church and how he thought they could accomplish them. After some discussion and clarification, they enthusiastically endorsed the new agenda and pledged themselves to doing all they could to accomplish it.

After a few weeks, though, the pastor was discouraged with the progress they were making on the accepted goals, and it seemed increasingly more difficult to accomplish anything. After much inquiry, listening, and probing of the leadership, he found the trouble. He had not enlisted the support of the informal network, the "fathers" and "mothers" of the church. Those veterans, who had served through the years, in season and out of season, but who did not hold church office, had not been enlisted. The new pastor did not understand that they had been promoted to a level of influence that was above the formal church office. The pastor retreated, started over, took time to enlist this informal group's support of his new initiatives, and then went forward. He served that church for many years and enjoyed a very fruitful ministry there.

I saw this at Wieuca Road Baptist Church and how it made a significant difference in the life and direction of the church. When I first went to Wieuca Road, several strong laymen gave the church wise and trusted leadership. The church did well during their years. However, age and bad health began to take its toll, and these leaders stepped aside. A younger, more ambitious, and inexperienced group came into leadership. The older group did not retreat from leadership; they simply did what they could to guide the church informally from the background. I greatly appreciated this.

Some issue, now long forgotten, rose up in the church and caused more smoke than fire. It hit the floor of the deacons' meeting, and they were chewing on it to a degree all out of reason. After this had gone on for too long, an old, wise, very respected, and deeply loved deacon tapped his cane on the leg of the chair in front of him in order to get their attention. Then he said, "That's enough of this." That ended the matter. Not another word about it was ever uttered in the public meetings at the church. It soon disappeared off of our radar. There is no secret way to get the support of the informal leadership. Building good relationships with them is so obvious. Explaining to them your thinking and listening to their comments are important.

I was in a restaurant in downtown Atlanta, and I saw the pastor of a large mainline church in the city seated at a table with about five or six older people. He seemed to be working very hard to explain something. The atmosphere was friendly. He was very thorough and polite, but he was also intent on helping them understand some things about the church. Later in the week I saw him at another meeting we were both attending. I asked him about the luncheon I had observed. "What was going on?" I asked. "Bill, we are in a building program and a very extensive renovation program. It is costing us a lot of money, and I was explaining it to these old families in our church. If they are not fully on board for the whole program, we will not have the support we need." He went on to explain that in his church, the informal leadership was unusually strong. He is a wise pastor and has served that church for over thirty years.

Leadership is established when you first meet the church, including the pulpit search committee. When I was called to the Edgemont Baptist Church in Rocky Mount, North Carolina, the committee made several promises to Carolyn and me upon which they did not follow through. The first promise was that they would have our furniture moved by a reputable moving company. I was just finishing seminary, and this was my first church, but we had accumulated some nice furniture and Carolyn's piano was very special to us. When the time to move came, I was informed by the church that they had decided to send some men from the church to our house with a truck to move us to Rocky Mount. I reminded them of what they had clearly promised and that I considered it a breach of trust if they did not do as they had said they would. They relented, and sent a moving van. Our things arrived undamaged, including the piano. Also, we did not have a group of church members handling our things, which seemed like a breach of confidentially.

They had just purchased a home for the pastor and promised that they would have it painted and repaired before we arrived. When we got to town, I went by the store owned by the chair of the property committee to get the key to the house. He gave it to me and said that they had decided not to paint the house and that it could be repaired as we went along in the year. I held my temper, but I was furious at this further breaking of their word. "The committee promised the house would be freshly painted, and I will not move in until this promise is fulfilled." The painters were there the next day and were painting as we moved in. There were no negative repercussions from these two experiences, which turned out to be serendipitous examples of the strength of my leadership style.

Our family lived in a church-owned house for the first few years in Atlanta. Their way of managing the parsonage was to let a committee make all of the decisions. The committee was dominated by two men, one of whom managed a large group of rental apartments and houses. Our children were young, and Carolyn was making every effort to be cooperative with the housing committee, but they could not get it out of their minds that we were not the same as the tenants in their low-rent portfolio. One day as Carolyn was trying to prepare the evening meal with two screaming kids demanding her attention, the door to the refrigerator fell off onto the floor. It scared Carolyn and the boys terribly. When I came home, I found the family very upset. The boys were crying, dinner was burned because Carolyn's attention had been diverted, the contents of the refrigerator and freezer were spoiling, and the dog was barking. After I helped Carolyn get the house back in order and the boys under control, I called the chairman of the committee about the refrigerator. His response was the last straw for me. He informed me that he would be going out of town for a few days on business but that when he returned he would try to convene his committee to consider the matter. He was not sure anything could be done about the situation because the budget for property had been depleted due to other property needs. I was furious. "This is my family you're dealing with, not some tenant in your rental property. We have small children, and we must have a refrigerator, IMMEDIATELY. The old one cannot be fixed properly, and it is more cost effective to just buy a new one." He was adamant, "Bill, you'll just have to wait until I get back in town and we can do our homework, and then convene the committee." I did not argue any longer, but I bought a refrigerator that day and had it billed to the church. I never heard another word about it. The informal leadership took care of the political consequences for me.

After the refrigerator door incident, I made some leadership decisions for my family. The ministry was hard enough when your energy is focused on doing the important things related to the Kingdom. I was not going to use up my energies on matters such as refrigerator doors and house painting. To solve the problem, Carolyn and I decided never to have any more financial attachments to the church than necessary. We would not live in church housing nor would we drive a church-owned automobile. This takes away a level of unnecessary irritation and a level of petty control over the minister's family. Each pastor must solve situations like this for himself. This was our way.

Many well-meaning church members have trouble realizing that the pastor works for God and is paid by the church. They are accustomed by our culture to think that they can call all the shots because the pastor works for them, drawing his salary from the church.

I also decided never to go into business or to invest with church members. There are some pastors who have been very successful doing this, but I constantly hear of situations that have turned sour, and when it does, it backfires on the pastor. When that happens, it is always unpleasant, and some influential church members usually end up leaving the church. I made this decision after some very unpleasant repercussions happened to me after a business deal with trusted church members went sour. They left, blaming me for all their woes when, in fact, I had nothing to do with their financial troubles other than I had invested with them. The pastor is too easy a target for many people to pass up.

Also, never borrow money except from banks or other lending institutions. Never borrow from church members. Whatever your means happen to be, live within them.

There will always be some members who make much more money than you do, sometimes with much less education and ability. They make it a matter of priority to let you know that they are doing better than you are, and therefore you should follow their advice on every subject, especially theology and politics, as well as church governance. Don't let that get to you. I have been doing this for a long time, and I have observed that in every case, they have their reward, and so do you. God, in His providence, over the long haul, does take care of His servants.

The community in general does not know how to evaluate churches and ministers.

While in Bradenton, we built a new sanctuary that, at the time, was one of the showcase buildings in the community. While it was under construction, several young businessmen with whom I had been working in the Chamber of Commerce came by my office for a meeting and a tour of the building, which was not finished. As we were standing in the unfinished sanctuary, we could see how the building would look when completed. One of the more vocal young community leaders said, "Did you lead them to build this?"

"Yes," I answered.

"You could have done so much more with your life. Such a waste," he said.

Granted, this did not make my day; it did remind how the clergy is viewed by some laymen. As I have matured and reflected on this, I have come to the conclusion that, as clergy, we cannot let others define us. They will never really understand what we do and why we do it. We must get our satisfaction from another source. When you are sure of your calling and have found your own voice, this is easier to do.

It took me a long while to recognize the fact that the church rarely reacts in a logical manner. This was made clear to me in a very surprising situation that occurred when I was pastor of the West Bradenton Baptist Church. We were in need of a sanctuary and would meet in what was later to become the chapel. After much work and planning with the proper committees and architect, we needed a vote of approval by the congregation before we could sign a contract. The big night came, and the church met in the chapel to consider the issues surrounding the new building and its considerable cost. The cost would be about three times our annual budget. It would also be one of the largest buildings in our town. The people wanted the new building very badly, and they came to register their approval. The presentation by church leaders took about fifteen minutes, and then the floor was open for questions. The only questions were for clarification of matters the presentation had not made clear. When the vote was taken, it was unanimous. The entire process had taken only twenty minutes. We left, rejoicing at the sense of unity within the congregation.

All was well until we got to the finishing stages of the project, and then tension began to be expressed by the people. This stress was due to a concern over, of all things, the hymnbooks. Not the content of the hymnbooks, but the color of the hymnbooks. Somehow this became a serious subject in the halls on Sunday mornings and on the dinner party circuit. We called a special business meeting to deal with this. The meeting was well-attended, and the discussion was heated. It went on and on. As moderator, I had difficulty keeping the meeting under control. Finally, after an hour of debate, we recessed the meeting until the next week. The item of the hymnbook color was referred back to committee to present us with a report when we reconvened. When we met to hear the report of the committee, the people were still anxious about the matter, but they voted unanimously to accept the committee's recommendation. They recommended that we buy white hymnbooks. It all seemed silly to me. We voted to increase our debt substantially in twenty minutes, and it took two meetings to decide on the color of hymnbooks. I could think of only one reason for this situation: the people do not feel capable of making the decision about the big items, so they leave it to the experts or committee. But over small things, they had strong opinions and felt empowered to express them. I believe that this is why so much church debate is over things that really do not matter. You learn to live with it.

# 9

## FLEECING THE SHEEP FOR FUN AND PROFIT:
## RAISING MONEY

On a beautiful Sunday morning early in September, we were
beginning our first pastorate. During seminary I had determined
to concentrate on the classroom in order to lay a foundation for
graduate school. I had preached every Sunday as a supply
pastor in the churches around the seminary, and I had also had
the privilege of preaching many revivals each year throughout
the Southeast. Carolyn taught first grade in the little town of
Zebulon, North Carolina, seventeen miles from the seminary.
During that time, we lived an almost idyllic life. When I was
graduated from seminary, I wanted to pursue a doctorate at
Southern Baptist Theological Seminary in Louisville, Kentucky,
but the graduate school at Southern was in turmoil and not
accepting any graduate students. Teaching first graders had
taken its toll on Carolyn, so it seemed that it was now time to
enter the pastorate. After all, I was armed with a degree from
Southeastern Baptist Theological Seminary in Wake Forest,
North Carolina, and was ready to meet the world, the flesh, and
the devil.

After graduation, I was called to the Edgemont Baptist
Church in Rocky Mount, North Carolina. The church was seven
years old and had had seven splits in its young life. I was to be
the first full-time pastor. I had had a considerable amount of
preaching experience through high school, college, and

seminary, but that is very different from being a pastor. Now it was show time; this ministry thing was for real. As Carolyn and I were in the car driving to church to begin our ministry to the flock that God had entrusted to my care, we assessed their needs and were overwhelmed. They were meeting in a half-finished building on three residential lots in a working-class neighborhood in this eastern Carolina railroad town. We were filled with enthusiasm and some foreboding. They seemed to need everything from general organization to a decent place to worship. A building program was absolutely necessary.

I had taken the five days earlier to move into the study and to become generally acquainted with the church and community. As I was walking down the hall to the place the church was using for worship (a half-finished future dining room), Tommy Tilley, the church treasurer, handed me a check. As he handed it to me, he said, "This is your salary check for the first week. If we have a good offering, you can take it to the bank." I later determined that he was telling me the truth. The church finances were worse than I had been led to believe. They were a wreck. We did have a good offering that day, I cashed the check, and that conversation with the treasurer changed my ministry forever. The church needed to learn how to give, and no one had ever taught them to do it.

The Southern Baptist Convention had just developed a stewardship education program called the Forward Program of Church Finance. Its purpose was to educate a church in systematic giving. Signing a pledge card was an essential part of the program. This was unheard of in the churches in eastern Carolina, and when I proposed it to the leaders of the church, they quickly informed me that this had never been done in any church they knew about. However, they did determine that it was absolutely essential in order to guarantee that the church would have a future. We rewrote the budget, organized the congregation for the program, and launched the campaign in January. Pledging was to take place the last Sunday of January. In the meantime, I purchased every book I could find about church finance and every sermon I could locate about stewardship, tithing, and generosity. I preached eight sermons in a row about the subject. That's right! Eight in a row, Sunday morning and evening.

On the second Sunday of the campaign, the chairman of the program, who was the leading layman in the church, marched into my office before the morning service and threw all the leadership materials for the campaign on my desk and resigned. It seemed that his friends, who opposed the effort, had convinced him that he should resign. This would ensure its failure. I was stunned, but we regrouped and went forward. Pledge Sunday arrived. It was a bright January morning, the temperature was moderate, and attendance was unusually high. The pledge cards were collected early in the morning worship service and tallied in another room while the service continued. When we announced the total to the church, they were astounded. We had tripled in pledges the total amount the church had given the previous year. I have never seen a happier church. Those who did not want the church to do the campaign and had been talking against it at every opportunity were the first to celebrate the victory and brag to their friends and neighbors about what their church had done. The former chairman, who had deserted us in the middle of the effort, was taking full credit for the victory. For the first time, I experienced the truth of the Chinese proverb, "Victory has a thousand fathers, but defeat is an orphan."

From that moment on, I determined that I would never let a church evade its stewardship responsibilities. Part of every pastor's responsibility, given by God, is to teach His church biblical stewardship. I have tried to do this through the years.

Some efforts have not been as successful as that first one, some have been even better, but they have all benefited the church.

Jesus taught his disciples that they could not serve God and mammon. We gloss over it in our teaching and preaching, but it is absolutely true. Mammon is referred to as "unrighteous" by Jesus (Luke 16:1–13), yet we are to use it. The inherent unrighteousness of mammon is a hard pill for us to swallow. We so badly want to believe that mammon has no power over us, no authority of its own. When Jesus calls it unrighteous, He forbids us from ever taking so naive a view of wealth. This calls us to be more tough-minded and more realistic about our attitudes regarding it. I can remember from my childhood in Delray Beach hearing the pastor telling the church that the dollar has only the value we put on it, and it can be used for either good or evil; we determine which way it will be used. I learned that this was an extremely naive view. Mammon has already put a value on it: it is evil and exerts an evil influence on all who posses it. But we need money. Therefore, we must control mammon and convert it to God's use in order to not be infected by it.

Remember that Jesus told us that in money matters, "The children of this world are in their generation wiser than the children of light" (Luke 16:8). The children of the world know that money is far from harmless; money is poison, and if it is used in the wrong way, it can destroy us as few things can. However, once we conquer money and learn how to use it, its power is virtually unlimited. Money has power out of proportion to its purchasing power. The children of this world know this and can use it for noneconomic purposes. Money is used to corrupt people and bring about all kinds of evil. Money is one of the greatest powers in human society. Jesus would have us learn to use money without serving money. The challenge of the preacher is to help the people learn this. They must be challenged to seek the overthrow of not only the spiritual power of mammon but the spirit of mammon within us as well. The more we conquer money's evil side, the more money is used rather than served, and the more it is a blessing and not a curse.

My mind and heart were opened to this when I read *Money, Sex, & Power* by Richard Foster.[21] This is the best understanding of the power of mammon I ever read. He quotes Thomas Merton, "Money has demonically usurped the role in modern society which the Holy Spirit is to have in the church." When preaching and teaching about this, the pastor will confront many reactions in the church. However, Foster reminds us that fear is the main emotion we face from our people. What Jesus says about money flies in the face of everything our culture teaches us about money and the good life. His words challenge every advertisement we see and every consideration we have as the privileged people in this world. Ultimately, the spirit of fear must be replaced by the spirit of trust before we can be the disciples He calls us to be.

In teaching the church what Jesus says about money, the pastor must walk a very narrow path. There are some things I have gleaned over the years that may be of help in the practical matters related to this most difficult challenge. The stewardship education program of any church must have at least five elements in it. They are: information, involvement, inspiration, insistence, and integrity.

INFORMATION: Remember that Charles Spurgeon said, "Most people read with one eye and listen with one ear."[22] That is doubly true in a stewardship education program. Every effort must be made to make the details of the church budget clear and the procedure for pledging it completely understandable. I believe that this cannot be over-communicated to the congregation. Plans are generally more or less useless unless they are known to all who may be concerned with them. Lord

Montgomery, commander of the Eighth Army during World War II, made it a rule that the plan of the campaign should be made known to every soldier. I think it is essential that all of the church who will listen know the plans for the entire stewardship process, from the offering plate to the execution of the programs.

INVOLVEMENT: The more the merrier. The more people involved in this effort, the more ownership they have, and the greater the likelihood of its success. Everything from folding brochures to stuffing envelopes is essential and must be seen by all as a necessary way to involve many people.

INSPIRATION: Not only sermons and stewardship lessons in the Sunday school, but testimonies by church members and from those who have been reached by the ministries of the church should be highlighted. Giving is ultimately a matter of the heart as well as the head. Where is the money going? What are the results of the ministries we are supporting? Have the efforts in some way made this world better?

INSISTENCE: I was having lunch with a group of friends from another church several months ago. Their concern about their church was that, although they were in a stewardship education effort, there did not seem to be any urgency about it. They stated that no one was insisting that the people participate, the follow-up was not being done, and not a word was coming from the pulpit about it. They missed the urgency within the congregation about it.

INTEGRITY: We cannot be too careful with the handling of God's money. Every effort must be made to assure the congregation that everything is being handled appropriately. Designated money should be used as it was designated. Those who handle the money should be bonded. The church financial records should be audited by a responsible outside auditor. Procedures should be in place so that no one is ever alone with the money, and two unrelated people should take it to the bank. I believe that the pastor should never handle any money. If trust is ever lost, it is almost impossible to get it back.

This is a very important part of our ministry. Every time I have seen a spiritual renewal breakout in church, it has been accompanied by a freedom and generosity of the heart as evidenced in the offering plate. It is the work of the Spirit of God in the human heart that ultimately separates the stewardship education effort from fundraising as done by the secular world. The clearest barometer of the spiritual maturity of your people is their giving patterns. "Where your treasure is, there your heart will be also." (Matthew 6:21)

# 10

## THE PASTORATE IS A MARATHON AND NOT A SPRINT: THE POWER OF A LONG PASTORATE RELATIONSHIPS AND DEALING WITH A CRISIS IN THE CONGREGATION

I believe in the power of a long pastorate. When a church calls a person to be their pastor, in effect, they have only given that person the chance to be their pastor. It takes a period of time for the bond between pastor and people to form. It is impossible to say how long that period is, but I have seen that there comes a time when it is noticeable to both pastor and people that the relationship has formed. For the pastor, it comes in subtle ways. He may no longer dream of the church he has just left. Also, there is a shift emotionally as he feels that he is beginning to love the church he has, rather than the church he thought he had or the church he has always dreamed of leading.

C. S. Lewis, in *The Screwtape Letters*, notes that after a while, the new convert to Christianity begins to note the human issues around the church—the dandruff on the shoulders of the ushers and the squeaky shoes of the deacons. It is at this point that the new convert is most at risk. The same is true of the new pastor. At some point he begins to see the reality that exists in the new church, squeaky shoes, dandruff, and all. When this occurs, he can be certain that the church has begun to see the same thing in him. They are beginning to become accustomed to his mannerisms and thought patterns. They now see the shortcomings that were not apparent to the search committee. This is reality time. When this time is recognized and both parties accept it for what it is, then the real relationship can begin. This is much like a marriage. After a while, moonlight and roses become daylight and dishes. Until the recording technology changed, I always told people that pastors were like phonograph records—to get what you want on one side, you had to take what comes on the other.

There is an authority that comes in the preaching experience that is unique and can only be formed between pastor and people after a long period of being together. It happens when the pastor tries to help his people rather than preach great sermons. This bond is formed after the pastor has walked the halls of the hospital with the parents of a child going into surgery, buried the husband of a faithful Sunday school teacher, or helped a good family get back together after one of them has gone astray. You know you are becoming their pastor when your program initiatives have been torn apart in committee meetings or in church conference yet you still love them. Trust is not built in a day, and trust and scar tissue do not rise in opposition to one another. Trust and scar tissue rise and fall together. Scar tissue earns trust. The people feel that the pastor loves them enough to work with them in spite of the rough-and-tumble of church life, and the pastor takes them seriously enough to disagree with their ideas.

You will know that the bond has formed when it seems more like family than it seems an organization, when you are more concerned with winning the person than you are with winning the argument, and when you can agree to disagree on important issues and then work together to make it the most effective church possible.

I was in a discussion group with several other ministers,

and, as an introduction to the group, we were all asked to tell the group where we were in ministry, not location-wise, but spiritually and emotionally. One pastor related how an older pastor had characterized the stages of ministry to him. He said that there are three stages of ministry; pitiful, popular, and powerful.

The beginning stage for any of us is "pitiful." We stumble in the pulpit, preach things we have not experienced, try to imitate other preachers we admire, and, by our leadership and preaching, make it clear that we have not found our voice. We look like children riding a bicycle with the training wheels still on. We look as awkward as a teenager preparing to take the driver's test in order to get his license. Usually our churches are patient with us at this stage. "If you are green, you can grow," an old deacon told me early in my ministry.

In the "popular" stage, we are beginning to be noticed. Invitations come to us to preach, lead conferences, attend meetings, and serve on committees of various boards and agencies. These invitations are flattering and hard to resist. There is nothing more intoxicating than to be the guest speaker at a large meeting in which you say the right things, receive an honorarium check, and drive home feeling like the hero. Of course, it is easy to be a big-shot away from home, but when you get home, you still must take out the garbage and attend a budget meeting.

The "powerful" stage comes later in ministry. You have survived the test of time, you are scarred by the rough-and-tumble of parish life, and you've been there and have kept your integrity and protected theirs. You have survived! When you speak, your message has the voice of experience and authority as well as scholarship. Younger pastors seek your advice. It is at this stage the pastor becomes most influential.

I shared with the group that I had experienced ministry in three stages as well. But they were somewhat different. These three stages were most evident during the twenty-six years I spent at Wieuca Road. They were "son," "brother," and "father."

Early in my ministry, and especially in the beginning years at Wieuca Road, I was the youngest member of the staff, younger than most of the leadership of the church. They all seemed anxious to help me "make it." I was their "son," and they wanted me to succeed. They encouraged me, helped me, and generally guided me through rough territory, making sure I did not get hurt in church decision-making. The leadership also made sure that I was protected on the blind side. They protected me in the conversations in the community and from the minor criticisms that accumulate in the day-to-day process of ministry.

The "brother" stage was the most difficult time for me. The older leaders moved aside due to age and change of lifestyle and a younger group began to emerge. At first, I thought this would be to my advantage. However, I soon noticed that the protection the older group had given me was no longer there and that program initiatives were having more trouble being accepted by the congregation. After much prayer and study, I came to the conclusion that the main factor was sibling rivalry. In the Bible, brothers do not get along. Cain killed Abel, Jacob and Esau continued the struggle beyond the Garden of Eden, Joseph and his brothers were fiercely jealous, the prodigal son and his elder brother caused the old man grief, and the disciples of Jesus had their problems, trying to determine who would be first in the Kingdom. So it is in life. Most people will tell you of strained relationships with their siblings. Every parent has had to deal with his or her children's sibling rivalry, and I found it no different in church. One man said to me, "You always have your picture in the paper; no one ever notices me." I tried to explain to him that this represented publicity for the church, not for me personally, but he never understood.

If the pastor can survive the "brother" stage, it will not take long for him to receive the rewards that come with the "father" stage. I was working with a committee at Wieuca Road trying to rewrite the church by-laws. They could not figure out how to define the role of the pastor in the new document, which is a very tricky thing to do. The document they were trying to improve simply said, "The pastor will perform the work usually performed by Baptist pastors." When they consulted those who wrote the original document, they were given the wise counsel to leave the document alone because the duties are virtually impossible to define or to write out. I have observed that when this is attempted, no human being is capable of doing all that the job description entails, which makes the document useless. The committee at Wieuca Road finally asked my opinion. I told them that the pastor is a Father for the congregation. The pastor usually does what a father in a family does. How do you define a father? Parenthetically, I think the Catholic Church has it right in calling their priests "Father." The committee could not deal with this, so I suggested perhaps they define the role of the pastor as a tribal chief. They did not appreciate what I had to say, but neither could they write a satisfactory description of the pastor's role. I think Father is the best way to describe the pastor's role. Granted, the pastor may have to move through the other roles in order to become the Father of the congregation, but it can happen. When it does, it is usually after some years, and, of course, some scar tissue.

In order for this to happen, some definite steps must be taken by the pastor. It is essential that the pastor keep himself refreshed, not only in spirit and emotion, as discussed earlier, but also in ideas and outlook. It is easy to find a safe and easy way to do your work year after year. The pastor soon learns that the same program template can be used over and over with new content placed in it. This is easy but becomes boring. The worst sin for any pastor or church to commit is to be boring.

How freshness is achieved varies. A group of peers could be assembled on a regular basis, and pastoral concerns could be discussed as program initiatives and preaching themes. Seminars are always available. Some pastors have found a sabbatical helpful. I have found a series of visits to respected leaders in the community, in order to listen to their wisdom, has stimulated me. Prayer and Bible study are essential but should be varied or else this becomes dull and routine. There are as many suggestions for this as there are pastors, but the main thing is for every pastor to work it out for himself.

Another essential for a long pastorate is to have a resolution to the issue of the balance of power in your life and in the church. In the last fifty years, every church issue I have encountered, either in the church I pastor or in situations shared with me by others, has come down to two main issues: who is in control and what shall we sing? These are power issues. Each church tradition has a different way of sharing the power, and in cases in which it has not been dealt with successfully, chaos reigns.

Power's essence is stronger than sex, and it is the funda-mental ingredient of the American lifestyle. This is true of power in any form and in any organization, church or otherwise. In the political arena, Franklin D. Roosevelt had it and Harry Truman picked it up on the first bounce. Richard M. Nixon threw it away. Gerald Ford seemed genuinely confused by it. Lyndon Johnson loved it almost sensually, having learned its tricks from another Texas master, Sam Rayburn. Some see it as the seed of the devil while others see it as a gift of the gods.

The power struggle started in the Garden of Eden when it was discovered that God knew something and had something that Adam and Eve did not know or have. They tried to steal God's wisdom and power. Who would control the Garden of Eden?

Power is difficult to define. Roughly speaking, power is the ability to move something from here to there, despite obstacles. It is the capacity to cause change in behavior. It is invariably personal, and it is always in the context of some kind of institution. It can be exercised only by the decision or act of an individual. It is always personal, regardless of how it is acquired. Power is the essential, fundamental, basic primordial, primary issue. In church, it appears when the budget is discussed, when the pastor is evaluated, when the hymns are selected, when the church officers are elected, and in every meeting of church officers or the professional staff.

The power struggle is the ever-present shadow that falls across all that we do. It is hardly ever a glamorous commodity. Power is a bastard child, and those who adopt it possess a certain cold confidence in themselves and in their capacity to keep it under their own control.

Power thrives on confusion and inefficiency. Powerful people never underestimate the value of uncertainty and lack of order, for through this they gain control. Harry Truman, when he inherited Franklin D. Roosevelt's White House, was impressed with the lack of order and confusion that existed. Later he learned that this is what kept power in the hands of the president.

The pastor must learn that power is like muscle—its tone and strength depends upon regular exercise. The wielders of great power use it often; they make it clear that they and they alone possess it. They delight in an exhausting vigilance through which they exert and preserve their power.

The pastor soon learns that to use power means that he will not lead a nicely balanced life. The powerful take few vacations, have no hobbies, and keep power by never being away from it. In the exercise of power, the pastor lives on the razor's edge between his confidence in the Gospel and human nature as he experiences it in the church. Powerful people never share power, and there is never a clearly discernable second man. The powerful leader seldom shows much interest in retiring. It is clear that when the powerful leader makes a mistake, it is a big one.

Most pastors are conflicted by the very thought of exercising power in the ways I have described. Christian power, or the power of God, appears to be in stark contrast with the exercise of power by the culture. The power of God consists of a certain subtle, almost tangible wisdom, visible only in its results. We see this illustrated in the Bible in the stories of Pharaoh's army versus the Hebrew children as well as the giant Goliath versus the boy David. The power of God is invisible, as in the hymn, "Immortal, Invisible, God Only Wise." Living with and by God's power is to know that the power is channeled through a person already committed to God.

If we are to understand Christian power and its purpose, especially for the pastor, we must understand that the proto-typical model for this is Jesus. Let us say that a person commits his life to Jesus as completely as he can. Then he is drawn into conflict caused by human sin. As a Jesus follower, as well as a pastor, he is committed primarily to the victims involved. From this vantage point, the pastor has a perception and under-standing of the total problem and its relation to those who have the power that others cannot see. With what appears to be amazing courage, he confronts the power structure. Illustrations of this are Jesus before Pilate, Moses before Pharaoh, and Paul at Mars Hill. This power structure may be an entrenched group within the church or it can be organized opposition against the pastor from the outside. Before this power elite, the pastor stands. He is unafraid because he sees their vulnerability as well as their strength. They must directly or indirectly destroy him.

The power elite at Wieuca Road offered me a compromise

that was most tempting. "If you will preach our way and lead us as we see fit, then we will give you the best years of your life. If not, it's over for you." They sought to destroy me if I did not capitulate to their demands. Yielding to their demands would have destroyed me also. The powerful may win the first battle, but, as with the prophets, a seed is planted that grows and ultimately cracks the strongest institution apart. For inspiration, though, recall that St. Francis, Luther, Wesley, and Martin Luther King, Jr., each stood before powerful forces and did not sacrifice their spiritual integrity. Pastor, remember that your behavior, as revealed in a crisis, is the product of years of prayer, reading scripture, and trying to live in relation to God in Jesus Christ and by the power of the Holy Spirit and with His people in daily life.

It is interesting to note that if you check the references to the power of God in biblical literature, they always lead to the Holy Spirit, as well as suggestions of the seed growing secretly. This power is not easily discernable yet has a way of bearing much fruit. God's power is ultimately with the humble people of this world, the young Davids who topple Goliath, a slave people escaping Pharaoh's control, or the infant church dominating Rome.

This discussion of power may seem, at first glance, out of proportion to the other issues of the pastorate, but I strongly believe that it is THE issue in every pastorate. Once recognized for what it is, the pastor is liberated to deal with it. Machiavelli lives in a thousand incarnations in every organization that has staying power in a difficult world.

It is true that there are many pastors who have failed to gain power, at least partially because of their unrealistic view of it. Many other pastors turn away from it because they have no interest in it or feel that it is somehow beneath the Christian leader to exercise it. Power remains, however, a constant and, despite the accidental differences of its setting, looks the same everywhere. It is one of the coldest and least deniable aspects of existence and, despite movements to the contrary, seems likely to survive like a fine, dark mist forever rising above the human condition.

How do we live and minister in this situation without losing our integrity and without compromising our Christian commitment? I believe the pastor must maintain a Christian lifestyle girded to the radical power that comes in Jesus Christ. This reflects a deeper understanding of power from a New Testament vantage. We are leaders of a faith community, and this makes us a part of a new reality. The community has a new power, a revolutionary force, which is different from the power demonstrated in the political arena. There has been an interior renovation in this faith community that has freed it from the domineering, victimizing forces of power, and this makes us a humanizing force in this world. Jesus described us as salt and light. He called us to become part of the faith community whose task is to witness to the ultimate power of the universe, which is the power released by Jesus Christ at Pentecost—the power of weakness, the power of love.

The reverse side of this power is the power of darkness and death, the principalities and powers. Exercising power as a Christian leader is tricky, but there is no other way for us to function and still be a follower of Jesus. If we do not model this, the church will not live it. Our people live in a world that uses power in a different way. Our people learn the use of Christian power primarily from us. They observe how we use it in the everyday life of the church.

There is another issue that must be settled in the pastor's mind if he is to have a long pastorate, and that is the sexual issue. To be completely frank, many pastors are leaving the ministry because they have violated their marriage vows. There are some experts on this issue who contend that these pastors have a deep desire to leave the ministry and that this is their way of leaving. This may or not be true, but if a pastor feels that he must leave the professional ministry, the honest thing to do is to admit this and leave rather than wounding a church with a moral failure, betraying the trust of good people, and making the work of the next pastor more difficult. The new pastor will have to clean up the mess left behind and reestablish trust in the ministry if his predecessor has left due to personal moral issues.

Pastor, when you stood at the marriage altar and took vows to be faithful until death parted you from your spouse, this meant something. The decision to be loyal was a once-and-forever decision; the issue of infidelity was settled then and there. There was no "as long as I feel like it" implied or intended. Carolyn and I have found that if we let the church know that we love each other and that our marriage is strong, the church feels secure and the opportunities for indiscretions are greatly decreased.

The long pastorate is the ideal. Here relationships are formed that are for a lifetime. We are known for what we really are and not for what we pretend to be. Our lifestyle and our life intentions are tested in a community that loves us. We have not only shared joy and gladness with our people, but they have walked with us through the dark valleys that are a part of every life.

To stay a long time, the pastor must face up to problems as they arise and deal with them quickly. This prevents the issue from growing out of control. If issues are ignored and allowed to grow and fester, they infect the entire congregation and are much harder to eradicate.

The long pastorate gives us the opportunity to move from power to authority. Authority cannot be earned overnight; it must be given by the people. When it is, the pastor has moved to a special place, the most influential place one can reach. When it is given, people will listen and act on the words of the pastor because they choose to and want to. Authority is trust and confidence. If the pastor assumes authority before it is earned, he is on a sure road to disaster. The power of a long pastorate is that during the years of testing, strength for the pastor, and trust by the congregation is developed. This is stronger than all the Machiavellian power one can possess. When this happens, the pastor has the best of all worlds.

## 11

## How to Keep the Home Fires Burning: The Pastor's Own Family

### *By Carolyn Self*

When Bill suggested that I write this chapter about the pastor's family, I hesitated, because I remembered the limited number of books on the subject in 1953 when we got married. At that time, I was about to embark on the most important journey of my life, and there were very few books on the subject. Those that I found were no real help at all. They had been written by the wives of successful ministers who had "made it." From what I could put together from these books, the authors led charmed lives. These women busied themselves giving syrupy devotionals to the Women's Society, leading in prayer (these were not bashful women), visiting the sick and not-so-sick, always having dinner on the table when the pastor got home (How did she know when he would get there? Time has no meaning to one who manages to capture his attention…), and raising the perfect children, who always happily complied to whatever the situation. Oh, I forgot to mention the perfectly clean house! What a burden to bring to a new marriage!

I took these books to heart, though, and really thought life could be that way. Silly me! It didn't take long for me to get a grip, and, believe me nothing does it quicker than two children and an ornery church. So you can see why this is a dangerous chapter for me to write. I really would have appreciated some experiences that I could relate to, because I had no clue what I was doing. It seemed to me that I must be the only imperfect pastor's spouse. I even wrote out a prayer that would cover almost any occasion and transferred it from purse to purse so that when my mind and tongue went in separate directions, I could at least read my prayer. Now, at this age, I am a firm believer that all of life is a learn-as-you-go experience. Each day brings its own joys and interesting circumstances! Start each day with a sincere prayer for guidance and enjoy the journey.

In this chapter about the pastor's family I am supposed to address some situations that someone new to this arena may not be prepared for. I will do this, because they are numerous, but I also want to tell you about the unexpected serendipities, the opportunities that are priceless, and the invitations that are not given to just everybody. Whether we like it or not, we are in a special category … sometimes that is good, sometimes not so good.

Often I have found myself wondering how in the world did I get to this exotic place? Me, a small-town, bashful, ordinary girl from a family of moderate means but a strong family unit. Me, the person who was determined not to marry a preacher or chicken farmer (I had good reasons for both!), with an undercover rebellious streak and a tree-climbing ability that allowed me to be "above it all" and read about far-away places to my heart's content. Most of all, I did not want to live a boring, mundane existence. Well, I have to say that I have often been tired but never bored! Sometimes the unexpected comes from within one's own family as a result of outside pressures and lack of support from the church family. Reality hits with a vengeance. Roses are my favorite flower but they have serious thorns. To enjoy a beautiful arrangement, the thorns have to be cut off first.

That is a picture of life, and a lot depends on us as to how and when we learn to prune the thorns.

Many preachers' wives begin this journey with their own "calling" to ministry. That is not my case. I had always prayed that I would marry who God wanted for me, but I had a few conditions of my own. However, I fell head over heels in love with Bill before I realized he was one of those dreaded ministerial students whom I had refused to date. Well, here we are, fifty-seven years later, having survived unbelievable circumstances (both family- and church-related), and our relationship has never wavered ... much to the chagrin of one man who accused us of being too close (he couldn't get between us!).

Bill and I have had so many wonderful, exciting opportunities come our way, such as being part of the president's delegation to the inauguration of President Tolbert of Liberia; an official visit to South Korea to help negotiate the release of preachers being held prisoners there; visiting with missionaries all over the world, including leper colonies in Thailand, and our sons running with the missionary kids through rice paddies; our blond sons being separated from us in Tokyo; me falling in a creek and breaking my ankle while exploring alone the ambassador's garden in Burma, and on and on I could go ... each a story unto itself. My point is to always look forward to the next surprise. Be open to allow your understanding and empathy for people to continually expand. You'll be living in a fish bowl, but be on the lookout for unusual opportunities that will benefit not only your family but those whom you touch.

Among the things you may discover in parsonage life, and which could be bewildering to a young, unsuspecting, and innocent spouse, is that not everyone who tries to befriend you can be trusted and at some point may actually betray you ... and never look back. Try not to let those people know you care.

Remember to keep your lips locked. Those people are trying to get power by being your confidant (literally, that means "someone to whom secrets are confided"). If you expose your problems or talk about someone else, you become extremely vulnerable. I learned to find friends outside the church. Alumni chapters of your sorority, a community group with interests that match yours, and childhood friends who have proven themselves are all lifesavers. No church likes for their pastor or spouse to be part of a "clique."

When you are young and inexperienced, you can expect some older women to try to take you "under their wing" and make sure you become indebted to them. Don't get caught in the web of suggestions that you have to go everywhere you are expected because you are the preacher's wife. The first step to avoiding that pitfall is to know who you are. Be comfortable in your own skin. You cannot be all things for all people, nor should you want to be. You will find that in the long run, you will be appreciated by more people if you are honest. Your integrity is at stake here … don't lose it. All this is said under the assumption that you have learned to be charmingly, graciously generous with your interest and concern for the entire congregation, not just for one group. This is more easily said than done, of course, but remember that your first allegiance is to yourself, your spouse, and children.

Our first church made life difficult for us. There were several very mature, kind, and caring women, but for the most part the women, young and old, were unhappy and bitter, and they "knew it all." I was so lonely and felt abandoned. Bill was working and visiting 18 hours a day trying to make a decent church out of this renegade bunch of people. It was small and had had seven splits and several pastors in seven years. This was the back side of God's mountain. These were not my people. Yes, I'm saying that. If you know me personally, you know that I can't help but be honest. I just knew that God had plunked us down in his most forsaken place and left us to fend for ourselves. (Haven't you ever felt that way?)

Bill and I both learned valuable lessons there. There was precious little money, and as Bill said in an earlier chapter, if the offering didn't cover expenses, we wouldn't have money for groceries. So he was frantically trying to make it all work. In spite of themselves, after about three years, they became "Church of the Year" in North Carolina.

This was more of a miracle than meets the eye. Let me just say that I, in particular, became totally convinced that we were living in a town of very emotionally sick people when I went to a dermatologist after Lee was born. I was seeking help for my extremely dry, flaky skin, loss of hair (were we both headed for baldness?), and forgetfulness to the point that I was afraid I would forget what to do with this baby (I didn't know much to begin with). The doctor walked into the examining room, looked at my chart, and after determining that my husband was indeed a preacher, told me to go home and pray about it. How about that for a medical diagnosis! But I'm ahead of myself ... maybe I'm still forgetting!

After five years of marriage, Bill and I started our family, and both Lee and Bryan were born in Rocky Mount. To make matters worse, I don't do babies well. I had toxemia with both pregnancies, and Bill came close to being a widower. We were so grateful and blessed to have these two precious, tiny but perfect babies. My life was a cycle of bottles, washing diapers (no disposables), and hanging them out to dry either outside or over the furnace, all while trying not to lose my mind.

I had overheard some talk at the grocery store and knew exactly what the gossip was. One day, about supper time, a big black Cadillac pockmarked by rain turned into our drive, and out stepped one of the gossiping ladies. Then the tap, tap, tap of high heels, and there she was at the back door holding a huge tray. "I've come to bring you supper!" I did not budge or offer to open the door. We looked at each other, and to this day I don't believe I did this. I said, "Mrs. G., it's too bad you went to all that trouble, because I will not have your food in my house. I know what you and your friends are saying, and we will not eat your food." I turned around and went back to the breakfast table and feeding my two babies. I couldn't believe myself, but I sure felt better. When Bill came home, I told him what I had done and that we had better start packing. I can't remember his reaction except that he didn't seem surprised. We were soon doubled over in laughter at the picture of the little two-faced woman holding the big tray! She must not have told anybody, because it was never mentioned, and we were doomed to stay a while longer.

Even toddlers are not immune to the abuse of unhappy church members. Rocky Mount was where the barber, a very close relative of the most recent former pastor, was so angry and agitated that his hands shook and he nicked Lee's ear rather badly. It was all downhill and getting more slippery every day. We were *so* ready to leave eastern Carolina and any place with "Rocky" in its name!

What a blessing when we were called to the West Bradenton Baptist Church in the lovely Bradenton/Sarasota area of Florida. Bryan was nine months old, and Lee was two years and four months old—a great age and a good place for an active family. There was a sanctuary to be built, and we were busy, but the stress level was manageable and life was more normal (whatever that is!). This is where I found an active chapter of my sorority with many young women near my age, none of whom were in our church. It was nice to be accepted by these women, who were compatible and let me be myself. Through this association and Bill's participation in civic activities I made other friends, one of whom became like a sister to me. I still miss and grieve for Martha, who died of colon cancer in her early forties.

I encourage you to develop your close friends outside the church. You have to be "friends" with everybody in your church, but for the most part, you cannot ever really relax and let your hair down. Any confidences will likely be misinterpreted, and when you least expect it, they will come back to haunt you.

There is a scripture that I think we need to read every day for courage as well as comfort. First Corinthians 6:17–19 instructs us to watch out for and be "on guard against people who cause divisions and put obstacles in our way ... by smooth talk and flattery, deceiving naive people!" If you haven't already experienced that, open your eyes and ears.

Something else that clergy couples need to beware of: *cliques!* Every church has a number of cliques. The bigger the church, the more there are, and your participation in one over the others is not good for you or the church. Whether you like it or not, everybody in the congregation wants to know you and your spouse, which is normal and understandable.

Fortunately, my childhood and adolescence provided good training for living in a fish bowl. My father was involved in running for political office as long as I can remember. He was the tax collector of our county for many years, but every election time meant that we hit all the political events: the fish fries, peanut boilings, speeches, and shaking hands and smiling while watching every word spoken! I was usually the one to accompany my father to these events because my brother was five years younger, and he and Mother stayed home. That is where I learned at an early age to closely observe the crowd. I'd find a good spot to watch the responses of the group and glean any little tidbit of conversation I could overhear. I learned a lot about people and human nature that could never be learned from a book. What great preparation for my adult life!

You surely know that the pastor's family *is* a politician's family. Yes, the pastor responds to God's calling, but you must never forget that the spotlight is always shining; you are public property. I discovered after Bill became pastor of a church (I hadn't expected this), that the pastor's family is a valuable source of sermon illustrations—valuable to him, that is. This is something that is unique to the families of pastors. Can you imagine what it is like to be an identifiable source of the sermon illustration with all eyes turned your way to see your reaction and the reaction of the children? There is no hiding place. I would surely have found it by now! I have to admit that it sometimes makes a point that brings home the fact that we do indeed live lives like everyone else and that we're very human, also. As long as your spouse uses discretion and is aware that this can be dangerous territory if he isn't careful, you have to just plaster a smile on your face. Pastor's children have a real load to carry, and some do it with grace and good nature, but some who are very bashful or perhaps of a difficult nature have trouble with this. Family illustrations may have to be cut or at least softened a great deal. Good luck on this!

Our years in Bradenton were very happy ones. It is a beautiful place to live, and we enjoyed being part of a growing community as well as a growing church. It was our Camelot, and it was also the Camelot time in our nation's history. The chairman of the Democratic Party was our friend, and he asked us to sit with him and others in the VIP section of Tampa Stadium for an exciting event. President John F. Kennedy would be speaking, the crowds were noisy and happy, and we were all hoping to get close enough to shake his hand. Only a week later President Kennedy would be assassinated at a similar event in Dallas. What an opportunity for us to have had through the hospitality of a friend.

Our Camelot was also coming to an end. Soon after that, we

were called to the Wieuca Road Church in Atlanta. Bill had always dreamed of living in Atlanta. It was a city of challenge, change, unease, and social unrest. It was 1964 when we arrived at Wieuca with no idea that we would be there for twenty years. Bill couldn't wait to get started, and so began our greatest time of challenge. It seemed that at times we were literally tossed to and fro either by the culture, our congregation, the integration issues and schools, the drug culture, the strange illness later known as AIDS, as well as the Viet Nam War issues. To put it mildly, pastors and their families had to struggle to keep their wits about them and not blink in order to survive Atlanta and the times. Many honorable clergy lost their jobs because of their integrity on these issues. We lost our older son in this social milieu.

As you can imagine, it is impossible to be prepared to face the challenges of all that I have mentioned, and when the teenage years also converged to join forces with the drug culture and the near death of the public schools, waves of despair almost destroyed us many times. As Bill has often said, the best advice is to "keep both feet in the stirrups and don't spit in the wind."

This section is written to give you courage to endure whatever comes your way. You just never know what will be next, but you can count on another storm coming.

The things that we experienced at Wieuca Road ranged from extremely good, kind, and sweet people and some exciting and unusual opportunities to be associated with religious leaders of all creeds and colors as well as heads of governments to the unimaginable tragedy of losing our older son, Lee, to the drug culture. We used everything possible to save him, but he continued to make very bad choices. Only recently has there been a change and a return to a more normal relationship. All those years were stolen from us, not to mention the toll that our son Bryan paid. It was not easy growing up in our family. It was hard not to lose hope along the way.

We are not making up excuses or being accusative, but you need to be aware of how some sensitive and difficult children can suffer at the hands of deacons, Sunday school teachers, and church peers. Never forget that those who claim the title "professional" in any walk of life may not be so professional when tempted to get at the pastor through the children. Not only were our sons tormented by adults while playing basketball (they refused to endure that after several games) but also while being prisoner in the dental chair (I have a great story on that one!) as well as being lectured by the carpool lady. It would take a book in itself to recount the series of devastating events that led our family into our own personal hell.

During this time, Bryan grew up fast. He couldn't help but know much of the turmoil that our family endured from about the time that Lee was in the sixth grade and he was in the fourth. He shouldered the responsibility of becoming "caretaker" of the family as best he could. One of the resourceful things that he did will surprise a lot of people. No one knew that at the end of the church service, while the last Amen was being said, Bryan slipped out and ran to the parking lot. At that time, the parking lot facing Wieuca Road was lined with large magnolia trees, so Bryan climbed to the top of the first one, where most of the people would pass when headed to their cars. Unknown to the people, he heard all the gossip and, most of all, what was being said about the pastor! Needless to say, our dinner table conversations were most interesting, and it was amazing how many people, not knowing this, were so adept at lying to us. However, Bryan learned a great deal about human nature that no book could teach, and he has always been able to know people for what they really are inside. That is not all bad!

As I have said, with some notable exceptions, we had a satisfying, productive life at Wieuca Road. In about our twenty-third year, Bill and I were both suffering from extreme stress, and he was rapidly heading for trouble: blood pressure, not sleeping, and all things related to stress. Finally, our wonderful family doctor had a heart-to-heart talk and told Bill, "Either you get out of this mess or I'll be seeing you in the emergency room." So we began to make our plans to leave. We agreed that we started our married life with no money, and we had managed to educate and provide for our sons. Even though we had all the extra expenses of prep schools and hospitals, we could start over. The important ingredients were still in place: our deep and abiding love and concern for each other and faith that somehow God would take care of us. We no longer tried to guess the next step; God's plan was always different and surprising. We resigned with some regrets but with a great burden lifted. We actually began to have some fun and could laugh again!

When First Baptist Church of Chamblee asked Bill to be interim pastor and then later to be the pastor to relocate the church to Johns Creek, I have to admit that I was not thrilled. But Bill felt truly called and was happy to have a place to preach again, so I made a valiant effort to make a serious attitude adjustment.

What a blessing this church has been for us! Even as it has grown, this church continues to be kind, loving, and open-hearted. The church has brought healing to our whole family. All of us were bruised and bleeding, and Bryan, Karen (our precious daughter-in-law), and I were on guard and very protective of Bill. You can understand that. Just before we made the actual move to Johns Creek, Bryan and Karen began to help in the Sunday school area, and we knew that we were all on the way to recovery, thanks to these wonderful people. This is what a church is meant to be like. We are grateful that God has given us this experience. My prayer is that you can also experience this kind of loving church. The lay leadership as well as staff leadership is unusually talented and dedicated to making sure we never forget who we are, why we are in this place, and that the cross, God in Christ Jesus, is the center of our worship and all we try to do.

In trying to figure out some suggestions for your life in the parsonage, I decided that the essential, number one thing is this: you must love each other with all your being and always nurture each other. This love and nurture has to be mutual. Commitment to God is first and foremost, but next comes your commitment to each other. I believe that the devil is always around the corner looking for ways to come between you and these two life-changing and life-giving treasures, gifts from God. You can overcome all odds as long as these are nurtured.

Taking care of each other comes in unexpected ways sometimes. As Bill said in an earlier chapter, he has always carefully protected himself from being accused of any kind of "flirtation" (for lack of a better word), but that does not keep someone from fanaticizing about him. There was an incident when I had to step in and be the protector. A certain woman had had several carefully monitored counseling sessions with him and began to flirt openly and cause Bill to be extremely uncomfortable. He is the kind one in the family, and he would come home from Sunday worship very distressed and embarrassed by her actions. After several weeks of this agony, I realized that he did not know how to handle the situation without being unkind. I asked him if he wanted me to take care of it, and yes, he did. And I did! Our Sunday afternoons returned to the normal recovery routine from Sunday morning. The important thing is to take care of each other, however the opportunity arrives.

As I have told our Nearly/Newlywed classes through the years, the basic ingredients of a good marriage and a good relationship can be found in Ephesians 4:29–32. Make these words, especially "kind, loving, and tender-hearted," the motto for your life. Maybe this is a good place for me to make another observation that I think is very important to the health of one's marriage. Nowhere in the marriage ceremony does it call upon either party to give so-called constructive criticism one to the other. I have heard many ministerial spouses say something like, "We don't want you to get the big head." You don't really have to worry about that. There are an abundance of people who will take care of that for you. Every time your spouse walks out the door and into the arena called church, there will be criticism in abundance. Too many people feel it is *their* responsibility to straighten him out. He needs to know that there is shelter from all that bombardment at home.

I know that Bill always wants to know what I thought of the sermon and the service in general, and I usually answer that before he has a chance to ask. It is *always* a good sermon (some are better than others, but I cannot know how many other people were especially blessed by that particular sermon), and there is always something to appreciate in every sermon. You never know who or how the people in the pew are touched by hearing God's word brought to them. Encouragement is what your spouse needs from you. Anyone who stands in the sacred place of speaking God's word to the hungry hearts of those in the pews needs encouragement and the knowledge that you are praying for him and for the service. That is a part of my own worship, and I feel that if the sanctuary were filled with praying people, our churches would have a more welcoming and spiritual feeling to visitors and members alike.

Don't forget that all our family members need affirmation and encouragement in order to do well in school, professionally, or at home. We desperately need a place of refuge from the blows we receive each day on the job, or school, or in a social group.

Also, Bill and I are partners. We take care of each other, respect each other, and have a lot of fun together. Not long ago, we were having dinner in one of our favorite restaurants, and a young man stopped at our table on his way out and introduced his fiancé to us. He had been the maitre d' in another restaurant for several years and remembered us, because he had observed that we always talked to each other. He said, "So many older couples never had a conversation with each other. They just order, eat, and leave." He was impressed that we seemed to enjoy each other's company, and he wanted to be that way too. So enjoy each other. Have fun together and never stop having inside jokes!

Bill and I are lucky that we enjoy the same things. If that is not your case, find things that you both enjoy, perhaps even developing some new hobbies so you have some common interests.

Even though life in the Stained-Glass Jungle is unique and challenging, I think that every profession, every walk of life, is challenging in its own way. It doesn't matter if one is a doctor, lawyer, teacher, salesperson, nurse, or computer guru, each family has its own set of issues, both good and bad. We are no different, except that we may have more resources available to us. Above all, always find time for each other. One or the other or both of you can be so consumed with other interests, even family, that you neglect the most important person in your life.

My wish and prayer is that you can glean from our experience some help, encouragement, and hope in times of trouble, and that you can recognize the good times and celebrate!

# 12

## THE VIEW FROM MOUNT NEBO:
## WILL IT MATTER THAT YOU LIVED AND SERVED?

It is easy to start something, but it is very hard to finish what has been started. Every home is filled with half-read books, photographs not placed in the family album, and projects around the house that will be finished when we have the time. Every pastor has a head full of books he has intended to write and enough sermon ideas to last him for many years to come. The tyranny of the telephone and the urgency of the immediate always cause these projects to be pushed aside.

Every life is filled with dreams that are never realized. In fact, if all our dreams have been realized, we have dreamed too small. The writer of the book of Hebrews also suggests this in the eleventh chapter, verse 13. Here, he discusses the people of faith who have followed (by faith) the call of God and their lasting influence, even though they never accomplished all they dreamed and saw. He writes, "These all died in faith, not having received what was promised, but having seen it and greeted it from afar, and having acknowledged that they were strangers and exiles on the earth."

Only Jesus could say, "It is finished" (John 19:30). The rest of us will only be able to say, "I lived by faith so as to fulfill my role in God's great plan." We are like a runner in a relay race; we do not finish but only run our part of the race. Not one of us is complete unto ourselves, but we need the other runners to make the work we do complete. It all comes down to faithfulness. Like the patriarchs of old, we see the goal, we run toward the goal, and in the end we hand the baton to another who will continue the race toward the goal.

All pastors should take great courage from Moses and his experience before the burning bush. He was called out of a comfortable existence, especially for an escaped murderer, after what is generally considered his prime years. He was called to perform an impossible task and given very few resources with which to work along with a group of people who were not so much concerned about a sacred mission as they were desiring of a way to get out of bondage. They, in many respects, were no different than the average congregation today. Never satisfied, always expecting more than they contributed, and expecting the leader to make all of their wishes come true. Moses learned what every leader has learned, and what every football coach knows: "In order for people to be what they have always wanted to be, they must be led to do what they have never wanted to do." He kept them moving by constantly reminding them of the Land that God had promised them. Their complaints are well known to all of us, as we have lived them in our own ministries. Moses interceded with God on their behalf, even though he was distressed by their behavior. It is suggested in the Bible that he became so weary of them that he moved his tent outside of the camp because he wanted some relief.

Now the whole enterprise was coming to an end; they were approaching the Promised Land for the second time, with a forty-year interval. The people wanted a new leader to lead them into the Promised Land and God concurred. Moses, exiled to a mountain on the east side of the Jordan, goes there to watch them receive their promise and begin a new chapter in their lives. He does not enter the Land, but just like the passage in Hebrews describes, he saw it but could not receive it.

Moses wondered many times, "Why didst thou ever send me?" (Exodus 5:22). Is this not like the cry of all of us as we seek some reconfirmation of our calling and of our lives? This will only come at the end of our ministries as we review what has happened to the people in whom we have invested our lives. When it does come, it will be for us just as it was for Moses as he viewed the people from Mount Nebo, where he had been sent to die. He saw that the plagues were over, the shadow of the death angel had come and gone, the sea of chaos had been crossed, and the murmurings of the people were over; their thirst had been quenched and their hunger satisfied.

Pastor, when you stand on your mountain, wherever it may be, and your people worship with joy and exultation in the presence of God, who sees, then you will know that He has truly sent you. But you cannot know until then, not with ultimate certainty. And when you do stand there, you will know that your life has been worthwhile. When you see the families who have survived the temptations of this world; the areas of the world that have been helped by the missions your people have participated in; when you see them safely worshiping in a house they have built together with a new generation finding the same Lord you have led their fathers to find, then you will know that it has mattered that you lived. When you see them resisting the temptation to cheapen the Gospel that Jesus died for while struggling successfully with the new issues that face each generation, then you will be reassured that it has mattered that you have lived and served. When you hear the applause of nail-scarred hands and the words "Well done, good and faithful servant," you will know that it *has* mattered that you have been faithful to the call of God to lead His people. It has mattered that you have lived and ministered.

# NOTES

[1] Hugh Heclo, *On Thinking Institutionally* (Paradigm Publishers, 2008).

[2] *Lectures to My Students* (Grand Rapids, Michigan: Zondervan) 154

[3] *Burnout: The High Cost of Achievement* (Doubleday, 1980).

[4] Roy Oswald, *Clergy Self-Care* (Alban Institute, 1991).

[5] *Minding the Soul: Pastoral Counseling as Remembering* (Fortress Press, 1996).

[6] Steve Kaelble, *Executive Health and Fitness*, 11 August 2004.

[7] *Anatomy of an Illness as Perceived by the Patient: Reflections on Healing and Regeneration* (Bantam Books, 1979).

[8] *Head First: The Biology of Hope* (New York: E. P Dutton, 1989).

[9] Allen Klein, *The Healing Power of Humor* (New York: Putnam Books, 1989).

[10] *The Trouble with the Church: A Call for Renewal* (New York: Harper and Row, 1965).

[11] *The Protestant Parish Minister: A Behavioral Science Interpretation* (Society for the Scientific Study of Religion, 1985).

[12] *The Joy of Preaching* (Grand Rapids, Michigan: Kregal Publications, 1989) 9.

[13] *Communion through Preaching* [New York: Scribner, 1952) 12.

[14] *Positive Preaching and the Modern Mind,* London, 1907. Quoted in Frank Colquhoun, *Christ's Ambassadors: The Priority of Preaching* (London: Westminster Press, 1965) 29.

[15] *Prayer and Preaching* (London: SCM, 1964) 65.

[16] Quoted in John Killinger, *The Centrality of Preaching in the Total*

*Task of the Ministry* [Word Publishing, 1969, 1.

[17] *The Word God Sent* (Harper & Row, 1965) xi.

[18] C. H. Spurgeon, *The Wicked Man's Life, Funeral, and Epitaph: A Sermon* (Music Hall, Royal Surrey Gardens, 1858).

[19] *How to Be Pentecostal Without Speaking in Tongues* (Word Publishing, 1991.

[20] *Christian Ethics Today,* Summer 2010: 7.

[21] Richard Foster, *Money, Sex, & Power* (New York: Harper & Row, 1985).

[22] *Lectures to My Students* (Grand Rapids, Michigan: Zondervan, 1958) 321.